A CHILD IN BLAIR HOUSE

1926 – 1942

MEMOIR

By

Laura Blair Marvel

ISBN: 1-4033-5653-X (e-book)
ISBN: 1-4033-5654-8 (Paperback)

This book is printed on acid free paper.

1stBooks – rev. 02/03/03

TABLE OF CONTENTS

DEDICATION

Dedicated to my five sons: Edwin P. Boggs III, George T. Boggs, Peter L. Boggs, Francis G. Boggs, and Robert B. Boggs.

PREFACE

My 17 Years in the President's Guest House

When I first came to Blair House as a little girl, I knew nothing of its distinguished history. I was four at the time. I had never heard of Robert E. Lee, Admiral David Farragut, Abraham Lincoln, or any of the other famous Americans who had shared meals and conversation beneath its roof. I was duly impressed by the building's grandeur, yes, but of its historical status I was ignorant.

That ignorance was soon removed. The master of Blair House was my uncle, Gist Blair, and when he and his wife, my Aunt Laura, adopted me in 1927 I became part of a Washington family that for over a century had exerted a major influence on our national life. Almost as soon as I arrived, Uncle Gist made me aware of that influence.

He did so in a very personal manner, taking me by the hand and walking me around his Blair House study and telling me stories about the mementos it contained. Because of the intimate associations that the Blairs had had with various American Presidents—and because my aunt and uncle were avid antique collectors—the house was full of historical memorabilia, and Uncle used his "props" to good effect in educating his young niece about her country's past. I first learned about "General Andrew Jackson," for example, because Uncle Gist owned the seventh president's cane. Back in the 1830s, ties between the Jackson and Blair families had been strong, and when Andrew Jackson died, the Blairs acquired both his private papers and his silver-tipped hickory walking cane. They gave the papers to the Library of Congress but kept the cane. During the years that I spent in Blair House, it rested in a corner of the library, as if awaiting the return of "Old Hickory" himself. When Uncle described the Battle of New Orleans, he first placed the hero's stick in my tiny hands. It brought the War of 1812 very close to home.

I recall his speaking, too, of Robert E. Lee. Shortly before he accepted the command of the Confederate Army, Lee was offered the Union Army at Lincoln's request. The offer was conveyed by Francis Preston Blair, the patriarch of the Washington clan and my uncle's grandfather. "Lee declined the offer right in this room," I can remember my uncle telling me, "while he sat in that chair by the window." And there were his stories of President Lincoln. These were the most personal ones, because Uncle had been born in Blair House in 1860, and as a child he had played with Lincoln's sons.

Lincoln himself would frequently cross Pennsylvania Avenue to unwind from the cares of office at Blair House, and Uncle used to tell me, with obvious delight, about walking into the front parlor and finding his father (who was Lincoln's Postmaster General) chatting with the President before a fire.

"They'd be resting their boots up on this mantle," he would say, as he walked me over to touch the spot. Or he would take me to the far corner of the room and point to a framed theater program. It was dated April 14, 1865, and it advertised a show called Our American Cousin. That was how I first learned the significance of Ford's Theatre in American history—from Uncle's copy of the program for that awful night.

Many of his stories were more recent, because he had been active in Republican politics himself around the turn of the century. In 1904, he had actually run for President. He was beaten in that contest by Teddy Roosevelt, who nevertheless remained a "bully" friend. As a consolation prize, Uncle used to joke, "T.R." allowed him to learn to drive a car in the back section of the White House grounds. He was on equally friendly terms with other presidents, especially with William Howard Taft. Taft was a frequent guest at Blair House, and my uncle had a raft of good stories about his relationship with that portly statesman.

Uncle Gist was my principal source for Blair House legends, but other people had their stories too. One of the most voluble and entertaining was my cousin Brooke Lee, the famous "Colonel Lee" of Maryland politics. Brooke used to tell me about finding John Brown's pikestaffs— the ones that were used to storm Harpers Ferry—down in the basement of Blair House; about Gist's aunt, Elizabeth Blair, having to wash cigar smoke out of all the curtains after each visit by General U.S. Grant; and about himself and his cronies, back in the 1900s, dressing every bust in the mansion, including those of Washington and Benjamin Franklin, in top hats before a formal dinner.

There was also our strange Cousin Percy, a debonair bachelor whom Aunt and Uncle tolerated as one might put up with a prodigal son. Although embodying the essence of Washington charm, Percy was also a serious drinker, and I recall him stumbling into Blair House many times at three or four in the morning, fresh (or rather not so fresh) from a long chat with one of the Capitol area's many madams. Percy knew every philandering congressman's favorite "girl," and the stories I heard from him after hours made me think that if Blair House represented southern gentility, Percy must be our Rhett Butler.

And of course there were the servants. Since I came to Blair House as a child, and since my aunt and uncle were so often occupied with the obligations of the Washington social scene, I probably spent as much time with the house's servants as I did with visiting dignitaries, political friends of my uncle, or other examples of the "right" people. Aunt and Uncle didn't approve, and they discouraged me from seeking their company. I couldn't resist it though: the "downstairs" crowd was such fun.

Uncle Gist's valet, Robert, was a pudgy, white-haired black man who had been born into slavery. Robert had been with my uncle since Gist himself had been a boy. Their relationship, an extremely close one, was a throwback to antebellum times. Robert used to take me roller skating, usually in front of the White House, until he was well into his 90s and could no longer stand the exertion. After that he would snooze much of the day, and it was one of Uncle's favorite games to creep up on him in his long underwear and startle him awake.

There was Marcel, our Parisian chef, who, after my natural father and Uncle Gist, became a kind of third father to me. When I first arrived he would sit me on his lap and tickle me until I begged for mercy. Then I would get a hug. Marcel was in love with my aunt's personal maid, "Esther"—who took charge of me—and it was a matter of some pride to me that they entrusted me with the secret of their liaison. If my aunt and uncle had ever known, I don't know really what would have happened—although, having tasted Marcel's veal, I imagine that even an old Puritan like my uncle would have been willing to make allowances.

There was our redoubtable head of staff, Victoria Geaney, a wonderfully efficient house manager who brooked no nonsense from any guest, no matter how distinguished he or she might be. She used to tell me, for example, how, many years after I had left Blair House, she once had had to reprimand the King of Yugoslavia when he was spending the weekend at Blair House. The king had thoughtlessly put his feet up on one of Aunt Laura's antique coffee tables. Vickie snatched Andrew Jackson's cane from its corner and smacked the astonished monarch over the shins. He took it with regal good grace, and even sent her a formal apology—but I always wonder if Old Hickory would have approved.

My growing-up years in Blair House lasted from 1926 until 1942. The following year, with Uncle Gist dead, the house was sold to the United States Government and became the official, not just the unofficial, "President's Guest House." Most of the people I knew in my time there—state governors and French governesses, heads of staff, and heads of state—have all been dead for many years, and this means that I am one of the few people still around who remembers what Blair House was like in its prime. Certainly, I am the only one who heard the many stories of the Blair family mansion from, as it were, the "horse's mouth."

This fact carries a certain obligation. The stories I've alluded to here, and dozens more like them, are my legacy. They comprise an oral history that stretches back to the Jacksonian era Blairs and that has been passed on, generation to generation, ever since. But they are not just family stories. Because Blair House has for so long been a kind of "second White House," its stories really belong to the people. As the last person to have lived in Blair House as a private citizen, therefore, I believe I have a kind of civic duty to tell its story. It is in my hands to pass that legacy on.

This is a particularly appropriate time in which to do so. For the past three years the stately mansion, which had fallen on hard times in the 1970s, has been closed while undergoing renovation. During this period, I have served on the Honorary Committee, as we have tried to recapture the special dignity of the building as it existed in my aunt and uncle's time. The restoration was completed in 1988, and I do not feel I am being immodest in saying that my memoirs will be able to offer visitors a unique perspective on Blair House's public and private history.

Because so many illustrious figures have made history within its rooms, Blair House is a national treasure—part of every American's cultural heritage. To me it is that, and much more. When I think of my 17 years in the "President's Guest House," I think of Jackson and Lincoln, and other 19th century historic figures of course. But I also think of Vickie and Marcel; of Madame Jeanne, my French governess; of Venable, our formal English butler; and of the dozens of visitors, long since gone, who made growing up at 1651 Pennsylvania Avenue so memorable in the 1930s. It is also their stories that need to be remembered, for it was they who made Blair House a home in the second quarter of this century.

Thinking back to my early days with Uncle Gist, I recall the strange sensation it gave me when I understood that this elderly gentleman had once played catch with Abraham Lincoln's sons. In telling me his family stories, Uncle was doing more than providing a link to the past—as important as that was. Like his father and grandfather before him, he was passing to the younger generation a sense of what history was about. In Uncle's stories, history wasn't battles and elections—it was people, real people like you and me—people who might have been called "Mr. President," but who still put their feet on the mantle.

Now it's my turn to pass his stories on. As I speak to a new generation of Americans—as I invite you in to what was once my home—I am trying in my own way to link the Age of Jackson, and the Age of Lincoln, to whatever may face our nation in the future. I like to think that Uncle would approve.

I would also like to take this opportunity to acknowledge the invaluable assistance provided by Tad Tuleja and Heather Palmer in making this memoir possible by organizing and editing early drafts of the manuscript.

Laura Blair Marvel
Greenville, Delaware
1988

CHAPTER I.*

Setting the Stage

Blair House stands across the street and slightly to the right of the White House on Pennsylvania Avenue in Washington, D.C. The block of land on which it stands, square 167, was originally owned by Stephen Decatur, Jr., the hero of the War of 1812. Stephen Decatur had Benjamin Latrobe, a Federal-style architect who had worked on the designs of both the White House and nearby St. John's Episcopal Church, erect a grand little mansion on the northeast corner of the square in 1819. By 1820, Stephen Decatur had died and it was around that time that his widow, Susan, began to sell off parcels of the square. Sometime within the next three years, several lots facing Pennsylvania Avenue were sold to Dr. Joseph Lovell.

Dr. Lovell was a fourth generation graduate of Harvard who in 1818 was appointed the first United States Army Surgeon General. This appointment necessitated a removal of the Lovell family from their home in Philadelphia to Washington, D.C. Since the move was meant to be temporary, for the duration of the office, rather than permanent, Joseph Lovell had an unknown craftsman build a modest home for the family. The downstairs rooms were given over to the necessary offices and entertaining areas and the parents and 11 children were crammed into the four bedrooms upstairs.

It was during the Lovells' residence from 1824 to 1836 that the home first acquired its reputation as a center of entertainment and as a meeting place for "the rest." Practically everyone of historical significance was a guest at a meal or a reception in the home at some time during the 12 years that the Lovells were in Washington. Mrs. Lovell was widely praised for her beauty, charm, and tact. Dr. Lovell was a marvelous conversationalist. One of the topics on which Dr. Lovell waxed long was the relationship between the weather and health. He charged all of his officers to make notations about the weather when reporting to him of illness and it was due to his efforts that a National Weather Bureau was eventually established.

Tragically for the 11 Lovell children, the parents died within a week of each other. The children went to live with relatives and the Lovell home, outbuildings, and all surrounding land were placed on the market. The buyer was my Uncle Gist's grandfather, Francis Preston Blair.

Francis Preston Blair was a Kentucky newspaperman whose fiery editorials in favor of Andrew Jackson were brought to the attention of the

President. President Jackson, who was getting bad press in Washington, D.C., decided that he could get more publicity in his favor if he established a "pro administration" newspaper and he decided that Blair was the man to head it. On Sunday, November 2, 1830, Francis Preston Blair arrived in Washington. He had met with an accident on the road and appeared at the White House in a bedraggled state, but the President welcomed him and set him before others, thus further winning the newspaperman's heart.

Due to both the excellent writing and the strong-armed subscription techniques, Francis' paper, "The Globe," became a booming success. By 1835, there were 17,000 subscribers! More importantly, Francis had established a secure printing house with a latch onto government printing contracts, so that he could establish himself in Washington securely despite the future changes in administration. By 1836, the Blair family was ready to move out of rented rooms and buy its own house. Francis initially looked at the Decatur House and Octagon, but his friends dissuaded him from appearing too grand and thus losing his "pull" with the common people. Blair settled instead in the old Lovell home. The location was close enough to the White House so that Andrew Jackson could visit daily and the well was widely reputed for its healthy water. Again, the downstairs rooms were reserved for entertaining and for an office, but the Blairs only had four children to work into the upstairs rooms.

Francis Preston Blair and his children continued to live at Blair House full time until 1845, when their country home was completed in Silver Spring, Maryland. With all of the children gone from home and because Francis was taking a less active role in his printing business, Francis and his wife, Eliza, moved permanently to their country home and rented out Blair House.

The first tenant of Blair House was George Bancroft. He was the first Secretary of the Navy and it was while he lived in Blair House that he laid the plans for the foundation of the Naval Academy. Another brief renter was Thomas Ewing, the first Secretary of the Interior. It was while Ewing was renting that on May 4, 1850, Blair House was the setting for one of the grandest weddings of the mid-19th century. Ewing's daughter married William Tecumseh Sherman in the Blair House parlors. President Tyler, Daniel Webster, and Henry Clay were among the guests present.

By 1854, there was a new generation of Blairs ready to move into the house. Francis signed the house over to his eldest son, Montgomery, who had graduated from West Point in 1836 and had established himself in St. Louis, where he administered the family land holdings and where he rose in stature as an attorney. In 1854, Montgomery was offered a position on the Supreme Court of the State of Missouri but decided that he would rather move home to Washington, D.C. to argue cases in front of the Supreme Court of the United States. Francis installed gas lighting in the home and Montgomery and his young family moved in. It was in this house that my Uncle Gist was born on September 16, 1860. By that time, Montgomery Blair was one of the foremost attorneys of his day. He was the man who had served, without fee, as Dred Scott's counsel. Montgomery was an ardent supporter of Lincoln, and less than three months after Uncle Gist was born, Montgomery Blair walked across the street to the White House one morning to attend the first cabinet meeting of President Lincoln. Montgomery was the Postmaster General of the Administration and so once again the downstairs rooms of Blair House were used exclusively as offices and reception rooms. The Blair family was growing, however, and in the late 1850s, Montgomery had packed his wife and children off for one summer to his wife's family home in Maine, and Blair House had had a third and fourth story added to it.

After the deaths of all of the elder Blairs in the 1870s and 1880s, Blair House was left jointly to the four surviving children of Montgomery Blair— Woodbury, Gist, and Monty, all Washington, D.C. attorneys, and Washington socialite Minna. This third generation of Washington Blairs was not as active in politics as their father and grandfather, but they were all active in the White House social circle. Gist also served as a delegate to the Republican National Convention in 1908 and 1912. Gist even "ran for President" in a very small way. He was delighted when his close friend Teddy Roosevelt won. President Roosevelt and Uncle Gist were such close friends that "Teddy" taught Gist how to drive on the White House lawn.

Monty, the youngest, was the first to marry, and after the advent of the second of what would eventually be a family of nine children, Woodbury, Gist, and Min agreed unanimously to give the family summer home to Monty while the three single children would remain at Blair House. Min eventually married, but she had no children and she and her husband continued to live in Blair House. In 1910, when he was in his 50s, Woodbury also married and his wife moved into the home. The space was starting to be a little cramped once the home had two mistresses and three masters, and family letters of the period indicated that things were running down a little as there was little agreement on how the house should be redecorated and who should pay. Min lamented in one letter to a friend that she was forced to borrow screens from the caterers when she gave a party in order to hide the walls on which the paper was hanging in shreds.

The situation was further complicated in 1912 when Gist, at 52, surprised everyone by bringing a bride into the home. He had loved Laura Lawson, also 52, for nearly 20 years and had stood by helpless as he watched her life nearly destroyed by an alcoholic husband. Finally, in 1912, Laura agreed to a divorce and the then scandalous divorce and remarriage rocked the Blair family. Min and Woodbury sided with the husband in the matter, writing to each other that Laura's long-standing affair with Gist was what had driven the husband to drink in the first place. No matter who was right or wrong about that, the fact remained that the three children and their spouses decided that they could not all continue under the same roof. In a silent auction, Gist made the highest bid for the house. Woodbury and his wife, Emily, built a grand home in the then more fashionable Dupont Circle area, and Min and Stephen moved into a modest home close to friends. Gist and Laura joyfully set about to feather their nest.

Laura had grand tastes. (Immediately after they took over the house she had reams of paper printed with the heading, "Mrs. Gist Blair, Blair Mansion.") Fortunately, Uncle Gist had the money to allow Laura to buy anything that her heart desired. Uncle Gist was also passionately interested in acquiring things for the house. All his life he had been the "keeper" of the family and his reverence for objects and their history had led most of the older relatives to will family furniture and mementos to him. He decided that he would outfit Blair House as a combination house and Blair family shrine—the headquarters of the family. In order to accomplish this to the satisfaction of both Gist and Laura, they spent most of the nineteen-teens and nineteen-twenties repairing, decorating, and purchasing. Their quest for the best in furniture and knickknacks led them to Europe several times. One of my most treasured possessions is a copy I have of a diary that my Uncle Gist kept during one of their jaunts to England and France. I think the few excerpts in the Appendix serve to paint a picture of the character of the dear uncle into whose home I was about to descend.

CHAPTER II.

From the Streets of New York...

While Uncle Gist and Aunt Laura were feathering their nest in Washington, D.C., I was living in a dark, shabby brownstone off of Third Avenue in New York, in a neighborhood that was the East Side version of Hell's Kitchen.

It was as far from Pennsylvania Avenue as you could imagine. The people my parents knew were mostly recent immigrants, packed four and five to a room in tiny flats. My friends' parents worked in factories and garment shops during the day, and in the evening they would gather on the front stoops, fan themselves, drink beer, and watch us play in the street. The rich scents of Old World kitchens—garlic, corned beef, sauerkraut—hung in the halls. The children—scrappy boys like my brother, Bob, and scrappier tomboys like me—would fill the streets until after dark, playing stoop ball and "prisoners' base" and kick-the-can. If you sat on a stoop and closed your eyes, you would hear snippets of Italian and pidgin German and Irish brogue.

Sometimes we could hear the sound of a scratchy radio or the clunking of horses' hooves as the junkman passed, and always there was the rumble of the El. Once or twice an hour it would come through, rattling windows and drowning conversation, and yet, in its own raucous manner, bringing the peculiar reassurance of distant thunder, and a bigger world.

I was born in this neighborhood in 1922, and I spent the first four years of my life here, with my natural mother and father and my brother, Bob. Our apartment was a second-story walk-up with a living room, two bedrooms, and a kitchen. There was a claw-footed tub in the kitchen, and a toilet in an alcove down the hall. My parents shared the bedroom in the back and Bob and I shared the second bedroom. We were perhaps a little less cramped than our neighbors, but it was still pretty close living quarters.

Like everybody in the neighborhood, we were suffering from hard times, but for us it was poverty with a difference. The Mangiones and the McCarthys along our block had been born into poverty in the Old Country, and they were doing their best to get out of it. Of my parents, only Mother was an immigrant; she had come from Ireland as a girl. My father was a Lawson from Cincinnati. His ancestors had been in America for generations and had acquired their social stature and money as founders of F.H. Lawson

& Company, makers of garbage cans and bathroom fixtures. The reason we were living hand-to-mouth was because of my father's one obsession.

I have known enormously wealthy men who squandered fortunes on alcohol and philandering and on the ponies. My father was the only person I ever heard of who ran through his inheritance by playing bridge.

It wasn't that he didn't know how to play. On the contrary, he was a wonderful player—so good, in fact, that he helped the world expert Ely Culbertson devise the rules for contract play that were standard from the 1930s into the 1960s. But my father played for high stakes, and he was obsessed. I remember my mother telling me, after he died, that even though he had graduated from MIT and had held a "respectable" job in the stock market for a while, the only thing he really lived for was four hands. And no matter how good you are at such a game, there is still an element of chance involved. That means that if you play it all the time, you're going to experience good times—and bad times. My parents, I'm sure, had their good times before the depression, before Bob and I were born.

The only stability our family had when I was young was provided by my hardworking mother, and there was a special irony in this fact. My mother, who was baptized Katherine Tracey O'Reilly, was a first generation Irish American, raised in poverty in New York by her mother. My mother had gorgeous Titian red hair that was so long she could stand on it, and she had beautiful legs. Just before she met my father she had landed a job as a walk-on girl with Ziegfeld Follies. This was too much for Cincinnati! When my father announced his intention to marry this striking showgirl, the Lawson eyebrows shot toward the ceiling. What would become of the family name? A dancer, of all things! With a brogue!

The irony was that, soon after this "interloper" was taken into the family, she was the one who maintained its respectability while my father, with gracious irresponsibility, seemed all but committed to undermining it. Since she had come from a culture where many clothes still were made by hand, she was a very accomplished seamstress, and in the period when my father's primary concern seemed to be what suit was trump, she was bending over a sewing machine at Saks Fifth Avenue from dawn to dusk six days a week so she could put food on our table.

My father did contribute to the household, although in a rather curious way. Since he stayed home most of the time, he took on more of the day-to-day chores than was customary for men in the 1920s, and I suppose you could say he was a little ahead of his time—a kind of déclassé house-husband. One of my mother's most vivid memories of that time, which she used to recount for me in later years, was of my father bending over a huge pot—not of soup, but of diapers boiling. First for my brother, Bob, and then for me, my father was in charge of nappy cleaning.

It wasn't exactly Cinderella and the Prince, but I've seen arrangements that were far worse than was theirs. They endured it, I suppose, for the oldest of reasons—because they were in love with each other. Certainly, my father was deeply smitten; he must have been to have so blatantly bucked the Lawson family plan. And my mother must have returned his devotion. To have put up with this charming ne'er-do-well, she must have taken the phrase "for richer or poorer" pretty seriously.

As bad as things were when I was born, however, a year or two later they got worse. It was at that point—1923 or 1924—that my father had a paralyzing stroke. The day that the stroke actually happened is my earliest recollection. I remember that early one morning I heard a cry and my mother running, and I saw my father on the floor. After that I have an image of him in bed, propped up with pillows and chain-smoking, with his bridge buddies gathered around him. I have no memory of him ever standing up, because after the stroke he never did. He stayed in the back bedroom almost constantly after that, surrounded by cards and thick tobacco clouds. We would bring him his meals and help him dress, and my mother would bathe him in the kitchen tub, carrying him herself as he was then bone thin.

Since he was always so confined, I don't have memories of walks in Central Park, or of swings and tickling games and playing catch, as most children do from their early years. I do recall that he was small and rather dark and that he had enormous, deep brown eyes—a characteristic, I later discovered, that the Cincinnati clan referred to as the "Lawson eyes." And I remember his pet name for me: "Lollipops." Like most kids, I had a terrific sweet tooth and it was my fondness for the stick candy that led to the term of endearment.

With the stroke, our finances went into a tailspin. My father's already erratic income was now abruptly and dramatically cut back because, although he could still play cards, he could no longer travel to find a game. My mother's situation became desperate. "The Christmas that you were three years old," she used to tell me afterwards, "I didn't have the money for one present. I used to walk the streets in front of the big department stores, looking into Bonwits and Lord & Taylor. Most of that December I spent crying."

Today, a young mother in such dire straits would have recourse to federal and state assistance, but this was in 1924, with "Silent Cal" Coolidge in the White House, and in those days, there was no such safety net. My mother did the only thing she could do. She wrote to her husband's wealthy sister to help us out.

I'm sure it was not an easy thing for her to do, given the cool reception she had been given by the Lawsons when she and my father got married, but desperate straits call for desperate measures, and so she approached my Aunt Laura. She was my father's elder sister, after whom I had been named, and she lived in Washington, D.C. with her husband, Major Gist Blair.

For a few months, I believe, they sent us money, and my mother balanced the books as well as she could with the help of this added income. But then Aunt Laura and the Major—who had no children of their own— suggested a temporary arrangement that would further ease the pressure on our family, and give them some pleasure in the bargain. They suggested taking one of us in.

That suggestion would change my life forever.

*   *   *   *

According to the original plan, it was Bob who was to go to Washington, not I. For some reason I have never been able to comprehend, Aunt Laura and Uncle Gist felt that it would be easier to take care of a boy than a girl. Preliminary arrangements were made for the Major to travel to New York to see "the boy" in our home, and work out the basics of his stay.

On the day of his visit, I knew nothing of the proposal. I knew we were poor, of course, but I did not know that our circumstances and Uncle's trip were connected. At four years of age, I didn't much care. All I really cared about that day, in fact, was playing on the sidewalk outside of our apartment.

Maybe it was being raised in a tough neighborhood, or maybe it was inborn orneriness, but by the time I was four years old, I was already a card-carrying tomboy. My idea of a good time was climbing the iron picket fences along our block. I hated dolls and I hated tea sets and more than anything else, I hated dressing up.

I was glad that on that particular day only Bob had to get dressed up. Two years older than me, Bob looked prim, proper, and completely uncomfortable in his black velvet pants and white satin top. For some reason, he had to stay inside and await the arrival of our visitor, while I was permitted the freedom of the block.

Taking full advantage of that freedom, I immediately got into trouble. I don't recall which one of the rough-and-tumble neighbor boys started the fight, or what we were fighting about, but I can imagine it was some unforgivable name-calling. I do recall hair being pulled and dirt being thrown and a good deal of pushing and shoving. Within seconds, I had made a complete shambles of my appearance. With my hair sticking out in 20 directions, my face smudged, and the front of my dress torn, I looked like one of the "Dead End" kids. In this sorry condition, I marched back to the house to tell my brother, Bob, of my adventure.

I found him sitting stiffly in the front room. With him were Mother and Father—predictably undelighted at my appearance—and an older man I had never seen before. Smoothing my hair and wiping the dirt from my cheeks, my mother uttered a small, plaintive sigh and introduced me to the visitor.

"This is our Laura. Laura, this is your uncle, Major Blair."

I had been hearing about "the Major" for several days, but nothing prepared me for what I now saw. Tall, thin except for his stomach, and extremely erect in his bearing, my father's brother-in-law was what an adult might call "formidable." He wore a crisp navy blazer and white trousers, and he balanced a straw skimmer on one knee. His glasses were gold-rimmed pince-nez. His mustache was short and clipped and white. His head was as smooth as an egg. He didn't look a bit like my slight father, or like any of the fathers in our working-class neighborhood. At four, I didn't know what to make of him.

Shyness was not one of my noticeable traits at that age, and to get a better idea of who this stranger was, I decided to get a closer look, so I grabbed an empty chair and dragged it over. Placing the chair directly across from the one that the man was sitting in, I climbed up onto the seat, brought my street urchin's face to within several inches of his, and tried to puzzle him out. Not the very best of company manners, but at four you don't think much about manners, especially with somebody who looks like a ship captain sitting in your living room. For several seconds, I just peered at him intently, inspecting the pince-nez and the mustache and trying to get clear in my four-year-old mind just what a Major might be. Or what an uncle might be, for that matter.

For a few moments, we stared at each other, me bedraggled and impish and highly curious, him immaculate and a little grave and, I'm sure, just as curious as was I. From the perspective of my mother and father and Bob, we must have looked like a scene from a Shirley Temple movie where the little moppet pouts at Victor McLaughlin. My mother didn't like our version of the scene. As I stood there, perched on the chair, I could hear her say over my shoulder, "You should get down now, Laura dear, you need to tidy up." I was about to climb down obediently, but instead I followed an impulse I can't really explain, but that was to alter my destiny—indeed, everyone's destiny—dramatically from that moment forward.

Esther, my Aunt Laura's Swedish maid, who became my companion at Blair House, used to tell me in later years that some people have an instinctual feel for their destinies, and that the so-called accidents of their lives are not accidents at all, but parts of a whole that was "meant to be." Maybe she was right. Maybe, as I stood there on that chair, I saw something in my Uncle Gist's face that told me he was part of my life's plan. Or maybe it was simpler than that. Maybe the distinguished stranger smiled at me, or winked, or said something that I don't now remember. Probably I'll never pin down exactly what made me do what I did. Maybe it was simply the same impulsive nature that sent me tussling in the gutter in my clean dress. I don't know. What I do know is that, all of a sudden, I threw my arms around his neck and kissed him. Uncle responded by picking me up and holding me.

For Bob and my parents, this was not terribly unusual behavior, and I doubt that they were surprised. Uncle Gist certainly was, though. "Flabbergasted" is how my mother described it later. After I had lived with him and my Aunt Laura for a while, I could see how this would be so. Their relationship was cordial enough, but it could hardly be characterized as affectionate. My Aunt Laura was always, I thought, a little too coldly formal for her own or her husband's sake, and I don't think he had experienced a genuine hug in years—certainly not in public. So when a grimy imp of a niece leaped into his arms, it must have come as quite a pleasant shock. He hugged me back—that much I remember—and although I did not know it at the time, at that moment the direction of my life took a dramatic turn.

I had no idea that my impulsiveness had derailed the game plan that had been made, but that is exactly what had happened. My mother explained to me later that, before he left that day, the Major had changed his mind. Maybe a girl wouldn't be so hard to raise. "Do you suppose," he had suggested to my parents, "we might make arrangements for Laura?"

CHAPTER III.

...to the Mansions of the Capital

A month or so after my uncle's visit, Mother took Bob and me on our first real train ride, on the old Penn Central to Washington. It had been decided by that time that it was I whom the Blairs would take in, so the suitcase that my mother brought along was filled with several changes of my clothes. Bob had come along partly for the ride, and partly to see where his little sister would soon be living.

As excited as we were about the journey—after all, this train was larger and far more luxurious than the El—we were not really prepared for the length of the trip, and one thing I remember most clearly about the day was that I was convinced it would never end. There were novelties that made the interminableness more bearable—like the ticket-takers with their uniforms and quiet smiles and hole-punchers which miraculously made confetti as they passed, leaving me to wonder at the many stops: Newark, Trenton, Philadelphia, Wilmington, Baltimore, and finally Washington. Miles and miles of open farmland whizzed by between the cities. New Jersey in those days was still the Garden State—in reality, not just in name—and to city kids like Bob and me, the sight of cows in an actual field and not just a picture book was a matter of some fascination.

And there was a novelty that my mother introduced. For some reason I could not fully understand, she insisted that I learn something called a "curtsy," and learn it before we got to Washington. So there I was holding on to a seat with one hand and the hem of my skirt with the other hand, dipping gracefully toward the compartment floor while the train rattled and swayed and Bob said "Oh, brother" with his eyes.

Being as physically inclined as I was, the peculiar technique did not prove daunting, and although I found it far less entertaining than, say, skipping rope or turning a cartwheel, my practicing it obviously pleased my mother, and so I worked on it between cow watching. By the time we pulled into Union Station, she admitted I had gotten it down pretty well.

It was a fall afternoon when we arrived. About all I remember of the trip from Union Station to Lafayette Square was that, compared to New York, Washington was a very muggy town. We traveled to Blair House in the Blairs' limousine, but I have no recollection of the ride. After a six-hour train ride, I was very likely asleep, or at least dozing, as the sights and sounds of what was to become my new home passed by outside the windows unnoticed.

I do remember getting out of the car at the steps of a gigantic pale yellow building, and being helped from the running board to the curb by a man who looked like a movie usher. This was the Blairs' footman, of course, but I had never seen a footman before. The only place I had ever seen a uniform like his—it was yellow, with gold shoulder braids and tuxedo tails—was in our neighborhood picture show. But no usher had ever helped me from a car, and this house bore no resemblance to a theater.

From outside appearances, it was not radically different from the house where we lived in New York. The windows were larger, and it was painted a dramatic pale yellow, not the dull brown that was common in our neighborhood. But there was an iron picket fence, just like at home, and there was a stoop with 10 steps—I could count to 10 by then—and there was the same kind of semicircular transom that I had seen so often in New York. This transom had the numerals "1651" painted in black. We followed the footman up the steps as he carried my suitcase under his arm. As soon as we stepped through the front door, I was awed by the beautiful marble floor and the high ceiling, and I knew I had never seen anything like this in New York.

The entrance hall to 1651 Pennsylvania Avenue was one of the grandest things I had seen in my short life. The ceiling seemed 20 feet high. The floor was black and white marble, with a runner of pretty blue with off-white patterns which began at the door and stopped at a grandfather clock. There was a marble-topped table on one side of the hall, and above it a huge gilt-framed mirror. The hall was not especially large, but it gave the impression of immense space, because off of it on either side were doors opening into enormous parlors. I glanced into the left one, but my mother pulled me to her and directed me to the room to the right where we were to meet Auntie and Uncle.

The room had oriental carpeting and the same high ceilings, a chandelier, a big fireplace, and a gallery of old political cartoons on the walls. It was the first time I had ever seen a cartoon in a frame. We were greeted by Auntie and Uncle, and for the first time I got a look at my Aunt Laura for whom I had been named. She was a small, prim woman of about 60, with dark hair and the famous "Lawson eyes." As she approached us with a faint, cordial smile, my mother leaned down and whispered in my ear, "Do your curtsy now, Laura, like we practiced." I did my curtsy. Bob did a little stiff bow, and our aunt and uncle smiled their approval. My mother was visibly pleased that our train ride drill had not been wasted.

This room, I was later to learn, had been Montgomery Blair's study before it became a front drawing room. Montgomery, Uncle Gist's father, was President Lincoln's Postmaster General—and one of his closest friends. The President had spent many hours here, unwinding from the burdens of his office, and he had often plopped his lanky frame down in the plush chair that now sat by the fireplace. I didn't know that at the time; in fact, I didn't know who President Lincoln was. And I had no idea, that first day, how well I would come to know this room—how many, hours I would spend with my uncle, listening to the stories behind those framed cartoons, or how, when I was not quite into my teens, I would make a discovery in the attic of a charcoal drawing of Lincoln hidden behind a trunk, which turned out to be the only one of its kind. All I was thinking about at the time was that it was a very grand room.

I didn't get very long to inspect it because, after the greetings and pleasantries were over, the adults sent Bob and me into a back drawing room—even larger than the front one—so they could discuss arrangements for my stay. There, my curiosity almost unraveled the plan that my affectionate greeting of Uncle Gist had brought about.

This back drawing room was filled with antique furniture, china, and silver, but, at the time, I didn't know any of that. My eyes went immediately to an item that stood off toward one corner—a beautifully crafted spinet piano. Our one extravagance in New York was my mother's piano. I don't know how we ever fit it into our tiny flat, but I do recall doing my share of key-banging. I went to the spinet with great glee.

My brother, who was all of six years old, but wise to many adult views, was reluctant to try out this new toy.

"Maybe we're not supposed to play it," he suggested.

"They didn't say we couldn't," I countered with what seemed to me to be impeccable logic, as I climbed up on the stool.

I started to bang away and, hearing no objections from the front of the house, Bob soon joined me. Things went along merrily until I realized that there was something wrong with the sound.

I don't know whether the Blair House instrument was out of tune or whether I was put off by its crisper, less resonant tone, but once we had "played" for a few minutes, I knew that something was "off." I did what any four-year-old would do in that situation. I climbed onto the piano stool, grabbed the end of the spinet lid, and hoisted it up with a flourish to investigate what was going on inside.

Unfortunately, I failed to check, before I lifted it, whether there were any items resting on the lid. There were: two large Bristol vases, which immediately crashed to the floor.

13

"Oh, great," Bob said, not exactly overflowing with moral support. He was two years older than I was, and as the silent partner in the crime, I guess he expected the worst.

The adults were upon us in a second. When my aunt looked first at the glass debris and then at me standing sheepishly on the stool, she gave a very good imitation of Pearl White going over a waterfall.

"Oh no, not the Bristol vases!" she shrieked. "Not the beautiful Bristol!" I thought that Bristol, whoever he or she was, was someone very dear to my aunt, and I confess I did feel guilty for a bit, wondering whose property I had destroyed. Years later, learning about antiques on Uncle's knee, I would discover that Bristol was an English ceramics center, and that the pieces I had transformed into rubbish were a matched pair of 18th century masterpieces that were then worth probably three thousand dollars.

Blair House, as I was soon to learn, was not the kind of place where you got spankings; discipline took the form of corporal punishment more prominent in "old days"—a "talking to." The talking to we got after the vase incident was a humdinger. It probably lasted five minutes, but it seemed to go on for hours, and the bulk of it was directed at me. This was logical enough, for Bob would be leaving the premises shortly, and my aunt and uncle wanted to make sure that the little terror being left in their charge would keep her heavily buttered fingers off the breakables.

The lecture made me feel for a moment that living in this grand and impressive place wasn't necessarily going to be a bed of roses. Everything, it seemed, was out of bounds. As long as I stayed here, my relatives told me, I wasn't to touch or even breathe on Mr. Bristol's china, or on anybody else's either. And if I had any question about whether a chair or other piece of furniture was all right to sit on, I was to ask them first, rather than just plopping myself down.

I stood there and took this tirade while Bob fidgeted and my mother wavered between sympathy for my plight and total endorsement of the house rules. She made it clear that, although she loved me and although she knew it was an accident, what I had done was very wrong. She let me know that, as long as I stayed here with my aunt and uncle, I should never go near their lovely things.

With their point made, they softened up a little and Aunt Laura, no doubt to reassure me that I was still wanted here, thumbs and all, took me into the front parlor and pointed to a bureau drawer I might open. Inside the drawer were some sugarplums.

14

"Those are for you and your brother, dear," my aunt said. "Now will you sit here quietly and have your sugarplums while we finish our conversation in the next room?"

"Yes, Auntie," I said. And we sat.

After maybe 10 or 15 minutes—during which time the sugarplum supply had been greatly reduced—the three adults returned from their talk. With them was a small, blond woman with bright blue eyes. She gave me a pleasant welcoming smile, and I had an instant sense that we would be friends. That sense was quite accurate, it turned out, for she was Esther, my aunt's Swedish maid, and during the years I spent at Blair House, she became more like an older sister than a maid. I learned how to read cards—not my father's specialty, but the fortune-telling variety—from her, and I was the only non-servant in the house who knew all about Esther's devotion to our chef, Marcel.

But all of that was years in the future. On this day, Esther had been called to provide an unofficial tour of my new home, and particularly, to show me my room.

There were two stories in the original Blair House plan, and a third and fourth floor had been added by Montgomery Blair. My room was to be on the fourth floor. To get to it, my mother, Bob, and I followed Esther through what seemed like an endless succession of rooms on the first three floors, nodding politely as she described each one briefly, like a tour guide. Hide-and-seek was one of my favorite games at that time, and as we wound our way slowly up the staircases, I was already sizing up the possibilities. There was a huge, multi-drawer desk in one room that looked exactly the right size to squirm under; there were poster beds with long, hanging coverlets; there was a Chinese folding screen in the dining room; and, in practically every room, there were draperies—not the skimpy curtains we had in our apartment, but real, heavy, floor-length draperies. For a four-year-old, the place was a paradise of possibilities.

The capstone of this introductory tour was my room. I was pleased to discover, first of all, that it was across the hall from Esther's room, and when I walked through its doors that first time my pleasure turned to amazement. Coming from a cramped New York apartment where I had had to share a room with my brother, I couldn't believe that this was all mine. There was a double bed that I was to have all to myself, plus a dressing table and a nightstand all in yellow with Chinese figures in a shiny black lacquer. There was also a huge armoire that would hold all my future clothes. There was a thick oriental carpet, a mirror, and a fireplace with a mantel. To me the place looked less like a child's room than like some exotic movie set. I was delighted to see it had no vases.

As if the inside of the room were not enough, Esther pulled the curtains back, giving me my first look across the street. I could see a huge white-pillared house that was grander even than this house. In New York, any kind of front lawn at all was a rarity, and this house had the biggest one I had ever seen.

"Who lives there?" I asked Esther in all innocence, and was told it was a family called the "Coolidges."

"Do they have a little girl, too?" I asked, and was briefly disappointed to discover that the answer was no. (The Coolidges' only surviving child, John, was 18 years old at the time.) But it looked like a wonderful house anyway, and I looked forward to a closer look at that lawn.

After opening the curtains, Esther left, and I was alone in my new room with Mother and Bob. While my brother and I explored its many attractions—Bob, I'm sure, with some envy—my mother unpacked my "visiting clothes" and put them away in the armoire. It must have been a terrible, wrenching time for her, preparing to part with her baby and juggling bitterness and sorrow and relief. Years later, when I asked her how she felt about it at the time, she always emphasized the "advantages" I was going to get—being able to meet a wealthy husband, and having all the things she couldn't buy me. But I know she felt more at the time. I can imagine the mixture of emotions she must have experienced as she settled me into this dreamworld miles from home and handed me over to my new family. I'm sure that her gratefulness for the Blairs' charity was tempered with resentment, and that her happiness in seeing me well "situated" was laced with guilt and confusion. I have no doubt she felt she was making the right decision—indeed, the only decision she could make, given the circumstances. Nor do I doubt that deep down the decision broke her heart.

I did not see the heartbreak that day. I can't recall any tearful farewells or, for that matter, any farewells at all. The last thing I really remember is my mother carefully putting away my clothes. We were in my new room, my mother, Bob, and I, and she was putting socks and underwear away. Then they were gone.

A psychologist would probably say I have repressed the memory of the farewell—that the trauma of parting from my mother was so severe that my psyche "refuses" to recall it. Maybe. But I think there's a simpler explanation. On that day that Bob and Mother and I traveled to Washington, my stay in Blair House was still considered a temporary expedient. I was to "visit" with my wealthy relations only until things picked up in New York. Formal adoption had not been discussed yet, and, in addition, it was well understood—by me, as well as by the adults—that my parents would be visiting me frequently, and that I would visit New York, too.

A four-year-old's sense of time, moreover, is hardly as sophisticated as an adult's. When my mother kissed me good-bye and said, "See you soon," I'm sure I didn't say or think "When, exactly?" It was probably enough for me to know that she was dropping me off here for a while, as she might drop me off at a neighbor's while she went shopping, and that I would see her and my father and Bob soon.

Besides, I had plenty to distract me from the potential trauma of seeing her leave. I had a palace to stay in. I had all the sugarplums I could eat, and my own room and a window that looked out on the White House. To me, the events of this magical day might all have been parts of a dream. I expected to wake up in New York very soon, and since I was always ready for new adventures, I resolved to keep my hands away from the china and make the most of this one while it lasted.

Little did I know at the time that my adventure in Blair House would last for 17 years.

CHAPTER IV.

Getting Used to a New Home

It was late in the afternoon by the time my mother had said her good-byes and time for my first supper in Blair House. Esther had taken full charge of me and showed me how to put things away in the armoire. She also showed me where the bathroom was—down the hall and shared with her. I was considered much too young to have dinner with my aunt and uncle at 7:30, so it was arranged that I should have supper brought up to me on the fourth floor on a tray and eat it in the playroom which was established down the hall. Esther would sit with me while I ate, and show me manners—of which I had very few.

The chef, Marcel, found it very hard to cook for a four-year-old. Everything was either too rich or too fancy for me, and it wasn't long before it was known throughout the house that I wasn't eating much of anything. It was Auntie who came to the rescue after phoning up some of her friends to find out the proper diet for a four-year-old. From then on my food was simple, but I didn't relish the spinach or some of the other vegetables! They were good for me, I was told, but I gagged on all of them. Peas and corn and carrots were okay, but not the rest. There was always caramel for dessert, homemade applesauce, ice cream, and the dreadful milk which I was forced to completely consume.

It was easy to understand how few things I really liked because I had never seen half of the foods before. If left alone for five minutes, as I often was, I would run to the toilet and flush most of my dinner down, and run back as quickly as possible so as to be seated and looking very innocent and very full. I was allowed to come downstairs for breakfast and eat it in the big dining room. I loved eating in the dining room, and I liked breakfast foods—hot cereal, hot cocoa, toast with honey, and one egg. I never threw this meal away.

Uncle Gist would always join me in the morning, as he had the identical breakfast. I used to be fascinated by the way he opened his egg. I had never seen a boiled egg in its shell, much less see someone pop the top off and eat the egg in the shell. He used to tell me how good a fresh egg really was, and never, never to eat a cold storage one. I wondered how one would know the difference. But, he knew! And many a time he would ring the bell for the butler and have the egg removed and another one brought forth. Reading the newspaper was a morning ritual for Uncle. Not one paper, but two; The

Washington Post and The New York Herald absorbed his time for several hours. He would sometimes tell me about the news. I didn't understand much of it, but he always treated me as an adult. He even tried to teach me about stocks and bonds during our breakfast time—that was the worst for me. I could hardly contain myself; I wanted to be excused so badly. Uncle was a very old-fashioned person, believing that children should be seated until everyone had finished their meal. To make things even more unbearable for me, he insisted that I accompany him to the morning room across the hall after breakfast while he read more of the newspaper. I would have to sit in a large needlepoint chair for at least an hour. Sometimes he would put the paper down, readjust the pince-nez, and just stare at me. I think it was just dawning on him that he had a little girl to rear and he didn't quite know how to do it.

Esther would appear before long and lead me away upstairs to see Auntie, who always stayed in her boudoir most of the morning. It was here that I was again taught to curtsy and shake hands properly, and to discuss what I should do all day long. Esther had already explained to Auntie that I needed lots of clothes, including underwear, socks, and shoes: the works. It was decided I should go downtown to the department store Woodward and Lothrop for the basics, and then up on Connecticut Avenue to a little French children's shop for my dresses.

I loved our trip to the big department store. I had never seen so many things on display. I was particularly interested in the little charge boxes that ran on wires all over the ceilings that would take the sales slip somewhere and a bell would sound, and down the little carrier they would come to the saleslady. I must have asked a million questions, as Esther kept telling me to be quiet. By nature I was a very inquisitive person. I liked to find out how things worked. This unfortunately got me into a lot of trouble on numerous occasions.

The uptown shopping spree was especially fun, as I was the center of attention. Auntie and Esther must have picked out dozens of dresses for me. They were all frilly, in crepe de chine, taffeta, velvet, and silk, and they all seemed to have long ribbons hanging from the shoulder to the hem line. How was I ever going to play in these outfits? They also bought me petticoats and Mary Jane black patent leather shoes, white socks, and a bow for my hair to match whatever dress I had on. Esther and Auntie must have had a wonderful time dressing their new little girl. Fortunately, I had pretty hair, and, according to them, a beguiling personality, even though I was rather naughty at times.

Uncle spent a lot of time at the Metropolitan Club late in the day. Often he wasn't home in time for dinner, and Auntie used to call the Club and ask for him, but was always told he had just left. She knew perfectly well that he was still there playing cards. The big game at the Club was solitaire. A member bought a pack of cards for $52.00 and at the end of the game, for every card left in the columns and not on the aces at the top, he would have to pay the Club one dollar. If he got rid of all the cards on all four aces, the Club not only would give him back the original $52.00, but would give him a new deck of cards, too. Then he would play again. In the end, a player usually lost, but he at least could keep the cards. There were endless packs of Metropolitan cards to be found in our library.

It was on one of these days soon after I had arrived that Uncle was a little late coming home from the Club. This time, however, he had stopped at the toy store on the way home. Since I greeted him at the door every night, I knew it was unusual for him to arrive with a huge box. There would occasionally be surprise presents in the years ahead. The first of these surprise presents was a full-size drum with all the fittings. What a present for a little girl! Auntie was furious and wanted him to exchange the gift. I was delighted. I banged all the way around the house—all the way to the basement to show the help, and then all the way to the top floor to show Esther. I was in "seventh heaven." Uncle thought it was amusing, but Auntie locked herself up in her room and wouldn't come down for dinner. If Esther hadn't come to the rescue and taken me and the drum to bed, anything might have happened. I was told I could keep the drum, but only if I banged it up in the playroom and then, not too loudly.

Another one of Uncle's unusual gifts for a little girl was a whole set of tin soldiers. I liked playing war. Uncle would sit on the floor with me and show me how to line up the armies against one another and how the attack should be made. It was hard to grasp all the military jargon, as Uncle had been a Major in the First World War, attached to General Pershing's staff.

Perhaps it was while playing toy soldiers with me that Uncle began to tell me of the military history of his family. His father, Montgomery Blair, had been appointed to West Point by President Andrew Jackson. Montgomery had been a competent but uninspired military student. He served in the Seminole War after graduation, and then resigned his commission to study law. The military stories about Montgomery's brother Frank fascinated me more!

Frank had been bounced out of three universities before finally qualifying for a degree from Princeton. Typical of Great Uncle Frank, his part in a rousing fight the day before commencement kept him from actually receiving his diploma. His portrait by Ulke hung in Blair House. It showed me a man with bristling whiskers who looked impatient at having to sit still long enough to be painted.

After he left Princeton, Frank went to St. Louis to practice law. He bought up land at a cheap rate and added further zest to his life by taking a quick jaunt to Mexico to fight in 1846. He ended up drawing up the legal code for the newly acquired territory. Back home in St. Louis, he wrote such sharp political articles that someone tried to kill him in 1849. In 1857, he entered Congress. He also fathered eight children and spoke all over the East Coast on behalf of the colonization of slaves.

In 1860, Frank campaigned actively (16 speeches in 36 hours on September 28-29, as an example) for Lincoln. When Lincoln called for Union troops, Frank raised the first regiment in Missouri and became Colonel. His activities during the War varied between his roles as Congressman from Missouri (in 1862, he became Chairman of the Committee on Military Affairs) and soldier (he raised seven regiments and was instrumental in keeping Missouri in the Union, and in keeping the Union in control of the Mississippi River).

Though all these events occurred 60 years before I entered the doors of Blair House, they were still alive to Uncle, and his stories and "props" made them alive for me. On the wall of the study was a photograph of General Sherman and his staff—Frank was in the photo. How the story of the famous "March to the Sea" came alive for me as I played with my toy soldiers, listened to Uncle, and looked at the photograph on the wall!

Although detractors in Missouri threatened his family and had him jailed and nearly court-martialed at various times during the War, Frank always rose to the top. Uncle would conclude his stories about Frank by telling me he had been just as old as I was when he stood with the whole Blair clan at the windows of Blair House on May 24, 1865 to watch Frank ride at the head of the 17th Army Corps in the parade of the Grand Army of the Republic.

I was much older when I learned about the post War years of Frank Blair. He began an earnest campaign for high office. Always one to rouse strong feelings, he carried two pistols to protect himself—presents from Derringer. But Frank carried the hearts of many people, as well. In July 1868, the National Democratic Convention named him the vice presidential candidate and running mate with Horatio Seymour. But really—no one could have won against Grant in that year. By the next presidential election, Frank had suffered a paralytic stroke—the effects of an active life had been exacerbated by alcohol. He died in St. Louis on July 9, 1875. The man who had had seemingly inexhaustible energy and strength died at only age 54 from a fall suffered while alone in his house as he had tried to walk from one room to another.

I know Uncle loved to have a "new generation" to whom he could tell his stories, but I do not believe Auntie would have approved of all that my young ears heard. In those days, little girls usually were protected from tales of war. I know Auntie definitely disapproved of the military gifts with which Uncle continued to provide me. Besides the toy solders and the drum, Uncle bought me a toy gun. Tomboy that I was, I loved to shoot at all the help!

A few months after my arrival in the house was Christmas. All of Auntie's friends knew by then that the Blairs had taken on a little niece, and that 1926 was to be her first Christmas in Blair House. A conspiracy was afoot. No "boy toys." "We must make this little girl like dolls and female things," Auntie must have wailed to her friends and to Esther. At last the big night came. I was allowed to trim the little artificial tree which was all the Blairs had, and which was always put in Auntie's sitting room. I hung two stockings on the fireplace mantel and was then sent to bed. But what child can sleep on Christmas Eve? I lay in my double bed listening to footsteps coming and going up and down the steps. There was a lot of whispering and giggling. Everything must have been hidden in some closet on the fourth floor. Dawn took its time coming. I got up several times and sneaked downstairs, but the door was closed. I was not allowed to peek until Auntie and Uncle were not only up, but had had their breakfast. I couldn't eat a thing, and I nagged Esther to death. Finally, I was allowed to enter Auntie's boudoir. I have never seen such a sight. I shall never forget how I felt. Two silk stockings dragged the floor, filled with fruits, dates, and small packages. The rest of the room looked like FAO Schwarz. There were dolls, trunks with the dolls' complete wardrobes, and little doll beds with handmade coverlets. I saw balls, a tricycle, and a little play piano with real keys—despite the Bristol incident Auntie felt that I should learn to play the piano as soon as possible. I was overwhelmed. I sat opposite Auntie and Uncle as Esther helped me open each present given by their friends and by Santa. Actually, it was too much all at once. I would have been happier with far less, but the Blairs were excited to have someone to have Christmas with them at last.

Auntie had been married before and had one son, Franklin Ellis, long grown up by the time of my arrival at Blair House. After her marriage to Uncle, Auntie had suffered a miscarriage, and they had no children. Uncle, a confirmed bachelor for 52 years before his marriage, was experiencing his first parental feelings at Christmas.

The Blairs always believed in having a family Christmas lunch which started at 12:30. I was allowed to join the family group and to sit at the big dining room table. Gist's nephew Monty and his wife, Ginney, were always there with their children, as well as the Breckinridge Longs and their daughter Tina, and Frank Ellis. Sometimes, especially later, we would have the Brooke Lees and their children. My first Christmas, the group consisted of Uncle's brother Woody and wife, Emily; Gist's nephew Monty Blair and family; my brother, Bob; Cousin Franklin Ellis and Katherine, his wife, and their son, Henry Ellis.

As soon as the group assembled, the butler brought in the cocktails on a silver tray. I was always given a small tomato juice which was slightly spiced and tasted so good. Since everyone wanted to know what I received for Christmas, Auntie took the whole group upstairs to see. My brother, Bob, had been placed with the Ellises as they had a son, Henry, the same age. That arrangement seemed to be working well. Though Bob was living in a different house, I could still keep in touch with him. He had a playmate, which I didn't have. I wished I did. Bob had been outfitted with little white satin shirts and black velvet short pants with white buttons all around. He looked adorable, as he was very good-looking.

It was soon after Christmas that I was told that Auntie and Uncle were now my adoptive parents, and my name would be Laura Lawson Blair. I never did learn to call them Mom or Mother, or Dad or Father—it remained Auntie and Uncle, but it warmed me that Uncle took great pride in introducing me as his adopted daughter.

My first winter at Blair House passed, and then spring, and I still did not have the governess of whom Auntie and Uncle often spoke. Esther was largely responsible for my care; however, Robert, the personal valet for Uncle, and as old as the hills, was still capable of walking me to Lafayette Park every nice day. We would sit on the park bench and feed the pigeons stale bread. I did not yet have any real friends, so I had nothing to do in the Park but sit and watch the people. Poor old Robert would nod asleep from time to time. It was a good thing I was too scared to wander off too far. It was not until the following year, after I knew a few friends who would meet us in the park, that I found the statues on the four corners of the Park. It was the first time I had ever seen naked males. We were all fascinated, and would spend a long time observing each one. Since sex had never been mentioned in my presence, I wonder what I thought at the time. Did I ask any questions at home? I doubt it, as Auntie and Uncle seemed much too formidable for that. In those days, you learned from your peers and hoped they knew what they were talking about.

My fifth and sixth birthdays were celebrated on April 6th at Grasslands, an unusual club out on Nebraska Avenue. It was a lovely old house and a charming place for parties and teas. I was allowed to have a few friends and we were taken out by our chauffeur for the afternoon and were served cakes dusted with powdered sugar. We would eat all available while Auntie and Uncle drank tea.

Like many Washington society people of the 1920s, Uncle and Auntie were affiliated with numerous clubs. Uncle, particularly, was both a "joiner" and an "organizer" and much of his adult life had been passed chairing committees and club meetings and attending dinners. Clubs grew even more important to Uncle as he grew older, for only in the safe haven of such places as the Metropolitan Club, the Alibi Club, and the Chevy Chase Hunt Club could he be sure to encounter old "cave dwelling" Washingtonians who shared his memories of the Capital in the last quarter of the 19th century.

To Uncle, who had been part of the "Boys' Club" founded by President Grant's sons, the recent, transient, and increasingly classless society of Washington was disquieting. Perhaps this is why he was so determined that my childhood should be filled with endless tales of "how it was" and why my childhood parties were held at "Old Guard" clubs.

CHAPTER V.

Summers

The Blairs always went to Bar Harbor, Maine each summer except when we were abroad. My first trip to Bar Harbor started the first of July, 1927. I had never been anywhere except New York, so this was a great event for me. Before we left, the house was slowly put to bed by Vickie Geaney, our housekeeper, who came in every day to clean. She was a wonderful person, and many years later she became the hostess for Blair House after it was bought by the Government. She was always my friend up to the day she died. In the 1920s and 1930s, her main duty was to close and open the D.C. House. This meant rolls and rolls of tar paper. The beautiful Aubusson rugs in the formal parlors on the first floor had to be rolled and tied in this tar paper, as well as each chair that was needlepointed by Auntie and Esther. All the heavy velvet draperies had to be taken down and hauled up to the fourth floor attic and laid on the long wooden table to be covered with tar paper. By the time our trunks were packed and shipped to Bar Harbor, the house smelled of nothing but tar.

The arrangement was that Auntie and Uncle and I would drive up in the Lincoln limousine, while the servants would come up on the special Bar Harbor express. Esther, of course, would accompany us in the car. No one warned me that it would be a long boring trip, or that I would experience car sickness. We were hardly out of Baltimore before I was green. I never actually threw up, but I felt, oh, so ill. I tried to curl up in the back seat and sleep, but because the roads were poor and the limousine rocked back and forth, I soon gave up.

Getting through Baltimore was always traumatic. The chauffeur always got lost, and Uncle would tap the glass with his cane and tell him to stop and ask. Have you ever known a man to be willing to stop and ask directions? Heavens, no! So around and around we would go up one street and down the next, row after row of white marble steps, and no way out of this maze. If we were lucky, Uncle would yell out of the window at the policeman directing traffic, and then after a long list of directions we would be lost again 30 minutes later. Finally, on our way up Route 1, we'd manage to make it to Philadelphia for lunch, always in the middle of the city at some big☐

hotel. At least I could get out of that terrible car and stretch my skinny legs and eat lunch, which made me feel so much better.

The afternoon drive to Trenton was filled with antique shops along the way. Uncle would spot them and bang on the window to stop immediately. I was always allowed to come in with them, as they wanted me to become familiar with antiques and whatever they were collecting at the time. I found this terribly boring; the shops were so cluttered and I never saw anything worth looking at. So much of it was breakable glass and china. In shops further north there was furniture. Uncle and Auntie would spend an hour looking at this and that, sometimes buying, but most of the time just looking. I always hoped after each stop that there would be no more antique stores before Trenton, where we were to spend the night.

The second day, we motored to New York, where we stopped to see my mother and father briefly. The visit was only for about two hours, as Uncle had the idea that I was his little girl and he didn't want my affections divided. This must have been hard on my mother, although it didn't seem to phase me until I was a lot older. I would kiss my father and he would always say, "How is my little Lollipop today?" His smoky room would send me into a coughing fit. By the time of my first trip to Bar Harbor, I felt that Auntie and Uncle were my two new parents, and I was glad to get away from the smoke and the little apartment.

Uncle, Auntie, and I spent the second night of the trip in New Haven, and then finally we reached Portland, Maine, where we stayed for two weeks.

Uncle had a lot of business with the Clapp Memorial Estate, of which he was executor. The Clapp Memorial Estate was set up in the will of Mary Jane Emerson Clapp, a first cousin to Uncle's mother. Poor Miss Clapp was always spoken of in hushed tones. She was born in 1820, the only child of wealthy Henry Clapp and his brilliant wife, Julia Dearborn. Little Mary Jane, fat and ugly, was raised amid many beautiful things—some of which were in Blair House in my time. After the death of her mother, Julia, in 1867, her father seemingly had become unstrung. Since Julia had loved botany, he ordered that a cutting of every plant, tree, shrub, and flower from the estate be placed in the coffin with her.

If this raised eyebrows in the town, they rose further when, after a year, father and daughter were still keeping all the curtains drawn in the house and making daily trips to the cemetery. This was excessive mourning even for the 19th century. Mary Jane's cousins (Gist's mother and her sisters) decided to bring Mary Jane to Blair House for a change of scene. While there, she "confessed" repeatedly to murder. She claimed to have murdered a grandfather she helped to nurse as a child and to have aided in the death of numerous children. It was impossible to take her for a walk in Washington because she often screamed that she saw children falling out of windows.

She eventually returned to Portland and lived in the care of a housekeeper and was looked in on by the local doctor. The town surely forgave her any of her picadillos when it became known that she left millions to the town. The poor of Portland are still cared for in part by the legacy of Mary Jane, administered by the Clapp Memorial Estate, whose office building stands on the site of her former home.

Perhaps in gratitude for her generosity, the town papers made little of her peculiar burial arrangements. Although she distributed many household goods and possessions to family members, the only suitable place she could find for her mother's prayer book, a pair of candlesticks, and six family rings was in her coffin with her.

Judge Thaxter was Uncle's best friend in Portland and his girls became my friends. I often would go and visit them on their little island for a few days at a time. It was there, when I was older, that I laid out all day in the sun without any protection and got the worst sunburn ever and had to be put to bed for several days, bathed in vinegar. My first sunbathing lesson was learned the hard way.

Living in a hotel for two weeks was quite an experience. I loved going down for all the meals and running around in the halls and inspecting the other rooms. It wasn't long before I became friendly with the chambermaids and helped them clean up the rooms. At least I hope I helped them, as I was still only five. I was good at pushing the carpet sweeper around. It was at the Lafayette Hotel that I spent hours with Esther learning to form letters. I would copy letters, newspapers, anything by the hour.

Sometimes Uncle would take me down to his office in the Clapp Building and let me talk to his secretary, Miss Sawyer. She was a typical Maine woman, accent and all. She gave me my first two turtles, "Amos" and "Andy," who lived for many years and grew so big that they could hardly be contained in their tanks. It was then that it was suggested that I give "Amos" and "Andy" back to Miss Sawyer, as she had the room for them. I hated to give them up, but the family was right; they were getting to be enormous and too much trouble. Many years later, I checked with Miss Sawyer and, sure enough, the turtles were still alive. I think they ended up outliving her.

After our two weeks in Portland, Maine, I somewhat regretfully said good-bye to the staff at the Lafayette Hotel and prepared myself for another long car-sick day. It took all day to reach Mt. Desert Island, stopping here and there for gas, lunch at Camden, and more antique shops, and finally we crossed over to the Island. We drove up Cleftstone Road to our cottage called "Cleftstone Cottage," and we were home at last. Escaping from the car, I ran all around, looking at the gardens and the beautiful green lawns until I suddenly came upon our gardener, John. He was kneeling by one of the flower beds, planting more flowers. I ran up to him.

"Hi! My name is Laura. What is your name?"

"Hello," said John. "My name is Johnny Abrams. Welcome to Bar Harbor."

"What are you doing and why are your hands so dirty?" I asked. He replied, "I am working to make the flowers grow. I also cut the lawn and rake the gravel driveway." He rose to shake my hand, but I withdrew and shook my head and said, "No, Johnny. Not until you wash those hands." I was told later that Johnny was hurt, but thought I was a very frank little girl—and quite amusing. I also noted that he washed his hands very frequently in the future.

My room in the spacious summer home was again on the top floor opposite Esther's room. It had a single white painted bed, a bureau, and a closet. The bath was down the hall and again, I shared with Esther. I loved these summers in Maine. I was soon taught to swim at the new Bar Harbor Swim and Tennis Club. Elmer, my instructor, met with a large group every morning at ten o'clock. My lesson was shared with Lois Thayer and her brothers and sisters, Louise Bowen, Elinor Pulitzer, Margo Finletter, Jane Cook, and others. We all learned to swim and dive, and eventually tennis lessons were included. The routine, which lasted for years, was that I would go to the Club in the morning. Uncle and Auntie arrived around noon and sat with their friends under umbrella tables. They all would talk and gossip, have one drink, and promptly at one, rise, collect their charges, and go home for lunch. How well I remember Mrs. John Thayer sitting either by the pool watching her children or at the table with Uncle and Auntie, knitting like mad. There was also Mrs. John Dorrance, dressed all in white, recently widowed; Mrs. McCormick-Goodhart; the Calketts; the Thorndikes; the Potter-Palmers; the Joseph Pulitzers; Mrs. Cochran; the Moores; and many others. Those years in the late '20s were very carefree.

Uncle's life in Maine was quite different from the one he lived in Washington. In Maine he always wore white flannels with a blue waistcoat and blue jacket, or sometimes a tweed one—and always white shoes. He topped this off with a straw bowler and he carried a cane. He wore knickers on his golfing days. The golf club was nearby and he loved the game. He also was interested in conservation. He spent endless time on committees dealing with keeping the paths and trails in good condition. He often attended meetings at the town hall in Bar Harbor. He was in close touch with "Ickes," who was a close friend of his.

Another very close neighbor living just across a patch of woods was Walter Damrosch, along with his wife and family. We could often hear Mr.

Damrosch practicing on his piano, which was in the garage behind the main house. His wonderful music would drift through the woods at all hours. His niece, Margot, became my close friend.

We had fun together, but she lived a very disciplined life. In the morning, she had to practice her piano for several hours; then she took German lessons, followed by a nap. Sometimes I would arrive at her door at the wrong time and be met by her governess and sent home.

Henry Morgenthau lived on top of the hill on Cleftstone Road in a beautiful home with a fine view—something we barely had. Today that site is occupied by a motel. The house was lost in a disastrous fire in 1948. Uncle became very fond of old Mr. Morgenthau although he was not friendly with many members of the Jewish faith. Adult conversation often would end with "but, he is Jewish." End of conversation. Every Thursday (still to this day) there was a luncheon just for men at the Pot and Kettle Club. Uncle wouldn't miss this for anything. Often the men would don chef hats and white aprons and do some of the cooking. They always had a guest speaker of some prominence. The issue came up as to whether they should allow Mr. Morgenthau in the Club. Uncle fought hard for him, and eventually he won the battle and Mr. Morgenthau became the first Jewish man to become a member of the Pot and Kettle Club. I remember a lot of heated conversation on the subject. It was so unexpected that a man of Uncle's age and background would do battle for a Jewish man, but when Uncle believed he was right, he stubbornly persisted. In Andrew Jackson's day, the press had said of Gist's grandfather, Francis Preston Blair: "In for a fight, in for a funeral." Uncle came by his temper legitimately.

Two of my favorite early friends were Elinor Pulitzer and her wonderful French governess called "Choo Choo." The Pulitzers lived on the sea on the other side of town in a huge mansion with one of the first indoor swimming pools, a billiard room, and a tennis court. It was truly an experience to be invited over to spend the afternoon with them.

Cleftstone Cottage, unlike Blair House, was rather informal and very comfortable. It had a very large living room with red fabric wallpaper and a huge red wool rug in the middle of the room, with very good oriental rugs all around the edges. There was a grand piano in one corner and massive furniture—black Spanish, very heavy with gargoyle feet, some delicate side chairs, tables, and the deepest sofa I had ever seen. As a child I used to play on this sofa, and jump up and down on it, hide in it, and curl up next to Uncle in front of a roaring fire. At night, the butlers would pull the heavy velvet curtains at the door to help keep the heat in on cool evenings. The dining room had more of the same heavy furniture. There was a small den for Uncle where he would spend most of the mornings, and it was there that

I received daily stock market instruction and behavior lectures. It was also there that we discussed conservation and made plans for trail walking or mountain climbing. This was also an intimate room for conversation with various members of the family as they would arrive for extended visits. It was also here that Uncle would call the help when bills seemed too high and he wanted an explanation. The only phones were in this room and in the kitchen, which had an old wall phone. Our telephone number was 144, and you had to crank the handle to get the operator. Every summer, the first thing I would do would be to get hold of the operator and ask who was up. She always would tell me about each of my friends, and exactly when they were due if they weren't already there. The telephone system has come a long way, but I loved the intimacy of the old style.

That first summer, I was still too young to take the riding lessons which came the following summers, so I often tagged after Johnny on all his chores. He taught me how to rake the driveway, which had to be done every day. I struggled with the lawn mower, which was too heavy for me, but I tried. I watched him sharpen the blades by hand, and rake up the cut grass, and tend to the endless flower beds.

It wasn't until August that Johnny realized that his lunch box was getting very slim indeed. He was sure his wife had given him a banana, or a cake or some cookies, but when lunch time arrived he seemed to be missing these items. I was the thief, of course. I knew he left his lunch box in the cellar by the old wood furnace. I would tiptoe down there while he was mowing the lawn and gleefully help myself to all his goodies. It was the day that I ate everything that the jig was up, and he went to Auntie to complain. From then on, he was allowed to eat lunch with the rest of the staff in the servants' dining room. I think Johnny inwardly thanked me for this, as now he would eat heartily and Mrs. Abrams would not have to pack his lunch anymore.

The wing that housed the staff's quarters was rather primitive. Beyond the pantry, where all the china and glass were stored and an ice box that contained 100 pounds of ice delivered several times a week, came the dining room. Since the staff consisted of Marcel, our French chef; Venable, the head butler; Al, the Spanish footman; and Carmen, the kitchen maid and eventually my governess, they needed a large rectangular table, which seemed to take up the whole room. The door to the back stairs opened into this room. A lot went on besides meals.

Al, the footman, was terribly good with the steel guitar, which he played a lot, accompanied with a better than average voice. As a child and even later as a teenager, I was very attracted to this part of the house. There was always laughter and story-telling, songs and games, especially checkers.

Marcel and Esther enjoyed card games, and others worked on the daily crossword puzzles. My favorite time to visit downstairs was around five o'clock. They would all be gathered to drink tea and listen to the radio or the Victrola. I loved to dance and often Esther danced with me. Unfortunately, Uncle was often lonely and bored around this time if he wasn't at a meeting or a club and he would ring the bell for one of the butlers to find out where I was. They would give me time to run up the back stairs before answering the bell. I would pretend that I had been upstairs all along and had not heard him calling "Laura, Laura," in a booming voice which I still recall these many years later.

Uncle usually wanted us to read together. As I got older, I did the reading. When I was younger, he read to me or just showed me his rare books. Uncle was an avid book collector and reader. At Blair House, his third floor "glass room" not only housed his collection of antique glass, but also had two walls lined from floor to ceiling with bookshelves. On the second floor, the two back bedrooms and the linen closet in between had been turned into one big "library."

Uncle collected books on art and on antiques, but mostly on history—especially family history back to the early 1700s. He also treasured books that had belonged to the family members he remembered of older generations. I used to love to open to the fly leaves where these dead and gone Blairs and Woodburys had written their names and hear Uncle's stories about each person. Sometimes, though, this would make Uncle feel lonely and sad, and I would want to get back to "downstairs" where there was always youth, laughter, and life.

Uncle hated my attraction to "downstairs" and would warn me over and over not to fraternize with the help. "You will lose their respect," he kept telling me. But they were my friends and were very protective of my welfare. I think I brought some joy into that part of the house, as it must have been very boring for them on the whole. As Auntie and Uncle grew more aged, there were fewer parties and very little for the staff to do.

The kitchen always fascinated me. Marcel was a pro, and whether at Blair House or at Cleftstone, he ran his territory with a steel hand. He terrorized us all, and no one dared to cross the kitchen when he was at work. We had a tremendous wood stove, which he managed to regulate by taking out different size rings. I believe anyone else would have burned everything up. The larder was in back of the kitchen with another ice box with another 100 pounds of ice. Despite these primitive conditions, Marcel always put out perfect meals, even if they were simple. He was much more creative in Washington, as it was there that the Blairs entertained lavishly until they got too old to continue.

I often used to sit in the kitchen late in the afternoon and help Carmen with the vegetables. As young as I was that first summer, she taught me to peel a potato, cut off the stems of the string beans, and wash the lettuce. Marcel would never appear until it was time to prepare the main part of the lunch or dinner. I used to try to watch him, but he would shoo me away saying, "If I show you everything, Miss Laura, you will soon take my job away."

Behind the kitchen was the pressing room, which was extremely busy in the morning hours. Uncle and Auntie's clothes were pressed daily, and a lot of the wash was done on the premises. The butlers and Esther were in charge of this. I was allowed to watch as Auntie felt that I should learn how to run a house and how to mend and iron properly. The coal bin was the last room in the wing; then came a drying yard. I cannot remember how clothes were dried on the foggy, damp rainy days Maine so often has.

Our trek to Blair House started around Labor Day or the following week. It was Johnny's job to put the summer house to bed for the winter, but since the main floor furniture was Victorian and the bedrooms contained painted furniture of different colors, there was not much work to be done. Often we drove home in the same fashion we had used in coming. We would stop in Portland again for a week or two, and then make the boring three-day drive to Washington. Sometimes the chauffeur would drive the car home with one of the maids. Marcel always drove his own car home with one of the butlers, while the rest of us took the train from Ellsworth. This was fun, as we had several compartments, and I shared with Esther. Having never slept on a train before, I loved the novelty, the dining car, and the porters who took such good care of us. We would arrive in Washington the next morning and be met by the chauffeur. Blair House smelled of moth balls and tar paper, but it was a clean smell, and everything looked so grand and beautiful compared to our summer cottage.

CHAPTER VI.

School Days and Europe

The time had come for me to enter first grade the year I turned six. Since Auntie wanted me to learn French as soon as possible, she entered me in the French Maret School on Kalorama Road. French was already well introduced after the hiring of my first real governess, Madame Jeanne. Of course, Marcel was French, as was a new chauffeur called Henri, who was young and much too handsome, but a good driver.

Henri was sometimes a thorn in Uncle's side as Henri had definite ideas of his own as to how to care for the car and how to drive it. Henri's job was to keep the car clean as a whistle at all times, as well as mechanically up to snuff. He was clever with cars and made many repairs himself. About the time I was adjusting to school in the first grade, Henri once had the Lincoln by the front door waiting to take us somewhere. The car looked beautiful— as shiny and waxed as possible. For some unknown reason, Uncle took it upon himself to inspect the other side of the car and it was filthy! Uncle was in the kind of rage in which he was often. He took his walking stick and hit poor Henri on the head. Why it didn't either kill him or split his head open I will never know, but somehow Henri survived. Henri, also in a rage, told Uncle to take care of his own car as he was quitting. What a terrible scene. Uncle always cooled very quickly. He apologized and begged Henri not to leave. After they made up, we went on to our appointment. I must add that never again did the car suffer a cleaning on one side only.

The first Lincoln that I remembered was a square-bodied car with an open front for the chauffeur. It was getting a little antique looking and had lots of engine problems. I heard Uncle and Henri discussing a new Lincoln—that it had to have a high enough door for Auntie to be put in and out of easily. They must have looked and looked to no avail, because the next thing I knew, Uncle had a car custom-built. It took a long time as even the interior had to be just so. One day the excitement rose in the house as word came that the new Lincoln was finally finished and about to be delivered. The car was beautiful! It was shiny black with a light gray interior, jump seats, a telephone arrangement to speak to the driver, and, of course, an open front. There was a black cover in case of inclement weather. When you rode in the back, you felt as though you were in a pullman train on very smooth tracks.

The only flaw, which almost got Henry dismissed, was with the new air brakes. One had to be extremely careful about putting too much pressure on them as the car would stop abruptly and all of us in the back would fly through the air and hit the window that separated us. Poor Henri tried so hard not to hit the brakes too hard, but on that first ride, every single time—bang! Uncle would be thrown to the floor, and poor Auntie would be dislodged as well. When we were safely delivered home after this shakedown cruise, Uncle got out of the car and started dressing Henri down. The more Henri tried to defend himself, the more Uncle lost his temper. Finally, Henri said, "Major Blair! If you feel that I cannot drive this car correctly, then you will have to drive it yourself." And with that, he flounced off in the direction of the garage, leaving the car parked in front of the house illegally. Since Uncle did not have any idea how to drive this new car, he entered the house and rang the bell for the chauffeur. Henri would not come—not before an apology was sent back by way of the butler. At last Uncle cooled down and did apologize, and ordered Henri to take the car to another garage and have the brakes fixed. We never again had to hold on to our seats.

Occasionally I took a trip to the garage, which was attached to the back side of the little garden. To get there you had to go to the basement and through a tunnel, up some steps, and presto—there you were in the garage wing. This wing also housed the servants' rooms. Though forbidden territory, I enjoyed a visit to talk with Henri and watch him wash the car, change its tires, and continually tinker with the engine. We spoke French, and he was charming, but he became a terrible flirt when I became a teenager.

I honestly don't remember too much about my two years at the French Maret School. I remember the classroom and my desk and the struggle to learn to read and write, but little else. I do vividly remember October 1929. I must have heard a lot of adult conversation about the big stock market crash, as I can recall the calendar on the wall and thinking that 1929 must be a very special year. I think Uncle took a small beating, but not nearly as much as the other members of the family. I think Cousin Franklin Ellis had a bad time of it, and Auntie had to get Uncle to help him out financially for a while. I don't think Uncle was very pleased.

In the summer of 1930, when I was eight, the Blairs took Esther and me to France for six weeks. We sailed on the "Isle de France" from New York. This was a real adventure for me. I was old enough to be allowed free run of the ship. I loved the gym room where they had saddle machines that simulated the ride given by a bucking bronco. If you got thrown off, you landed on a soft mattress. I played all the deck games and watched the horse races. I didn't always dine with Auntie and Uncle as they seemed preoccupied with friends of theirs. I often dined with Esther and Marcel, who was coming over with us to visit his family in Paris. The only thing I hated about the voyage was my cabin, as it was an inside one with no portholes.

Walking the promenade deck with Esther or Uncle was a daily routine. We often stopped at the stern of the ship to watch the wake, which I thought resembled a bride's train. The passage went quickly and we soon arrived in France. We stayed at Deauville, which was a beautiful summer resort with hotels lining the beaches and multicolored tents all in a row.

I had never seen such a huge bathroom as the one in my room. I thought the bidet was the toilet and used it as such, much to my embarrassment when I realized there was no way to flush it. Esther was quite annoyed when I went to tell her. Auntie and Uncle took many motoring trips from which I was often excluded. I played on the beach daily and that is all I remember of that trip. We sailed back to New York on the "Leviathan."

Back in Washington I was transferred to Holten-Arms, off of Connecticut Avenue. It was here that I started making fast friends, including Pat Protchnik, Anne Huidekoper, and many others.

It was during my eighth year that my father had his final stroke. One day when I entered Auntie's room I found her crying. Esther quickly intervened to tell me that my father had died that morning. I was sorry, but felt no grief, as I had only seen him a few times in recent years. I wondered what my mother would do now, or if perhaps she would feel free without the added burden of an invalid.

It was about this time that I started to feel sorry for myself. When I heard my school friends talking about their parents, I began to realize that my adoptive ones were getting very old. Esther used to find me crying in the bathtub for my mother. Auntie was distant. She was coming down with Parkinson's disease and her left hand began to shake uncontrollably. I used to come into her dressing room and watch Esther curl her hair with the irons heated on sterno, and apply her makeup and adorn her with jewels while Auntie held her left hand from shaking. She was still able to get around and had her usual weekly mah-jongg and bridge games. In the afternoons she would have her lady friends in and I would help set up the card tables and arrange the mah-jongg tiles correctly. I knew all about the little side tables for the ashtrays and cigarettes, as everyone smoked at these sessions. I never learned to play, but I would watch by the hour until tea was served, when I was allowed to have some of the little cakes.

The game that Auntie and Uncle used to play together in the evenings after dinner was Russian Bank. They kept a running score on paper which proved that after a year the score turned out pretty even. They taught me how to play, which was a good thing, as I took over later when Auntie could no longer lift the cards up.

My fondest memories of this time stem back to the hours spent in the library, which was, in fact, two rooms and a large closet that had been made into one large room, with two sets of windows looking down into the garden. When Uncle took over the house upon his return from St. Louis, he had the rooms made into one and brought in beautiful paneling and marble fireplaces. Red was the major color. A large red rug ran the full length of the room with a Chippendale library table in the middle, leaving group sitting space at either end of the room.

Bookcases lining the walls were filled with first editions and history books on Lincoln, Jackson, and the Blairs. There were also lots of books on silver for identification, as Uncle was an avid silver collector. It was here that I would sit way up on top of the overstuffed chair by the fireplace, behind Uncle's shoulder so I could look at all the pictures while Uncle read to me for an hour each evening before dinner. We loved Grimm's fairy tales and later, Mark Twain, James Fenimore Cooper, and Robert Louis Stevenson. Much later, we would enjoy Shakespeare together. I loved all the adventure stories. Uncle was a great reader and encouraged me to read as much as possible.

The A. Atwater Kent radio was down at the other end of the room from where we read. It wasn't long before I was listening to Little Orphan Annie, Amos and Andy, The Shadow, The Creaking Door, Lowell Thomas for news, the Eddie Cantor Show, and others. Now that I was eight, I was allowed to have dinner with Auntie and Uncle at 7:30. We had time to listen to the news and Amos and Andy before dinner was served. The butler always brought Uncle and Auntie their martinis before dinner and I had tomato juice.

It was in the library that Uncle would sit me down with the large silver book in hand, bring up a spoon or a tankard from the silver safe, and show me the hallmarks. We would look them up in the book to verify the silversmith and whether it was English or American. He had a tankard by Paul Revere, George II candlesticks, lots of English tea services, 18th century American coffee pots, and many other silver pieces, all kept in a safe off the pantry. One of the main responsibilities of the head butler was to see that all that silver was polished every day. It took a lot of rubbing to do the job right.

My favorite candlesticks were ones that had come from John Hancock. His wife had been a distant relative of Uncle Gist. After John Hancock died, his wife asked her great niece to keep her company. In her will, Mrs. Hancock left some family silver to this great niece. She passed the silver along to her own nieces, who were the aunt and mother of Uncle Gist. Uncle was very proud of being connected to the great signer of the Declaration of Independence.

For all his apparent worldliness, Uncle was a very religious man. From the time I first arrived until the day he passed away, he would walk me over to St. John's Episcopal Church to take me to Sunday School. Perfect attendance was rewarded with pins at the end of the church school year and, eventually, bars. Having won them all, I looked like a decorated general. Uncle was more than pleased that I didn't resist my early religious training. After Sunday School, I attended church with Auntie and Uncle and cousins Dorothy and Nathan Wyeth and Monty and Ginney Blair. We had a family pew then, so we could always know who was in attendance.

To follow up on his feeling of spiritual matters, Uncle insisted that I say my prayers every evening before going up to bed by kneeling in front of him. At first it was "Now I lay me down to sleep"; later, the "Lord's Prayer." To the end I'd tack on: "Please bless Auntie and Uncle and Esther and Madame Jeanne, and please, Dear Lord, make me a good girl. Amen." As I grew older, the list became longer and longer. On Sundays, Uncle would read the Bible to me and a prayer from the prayer book as a blessing before we ate.

Our Sunday lunches were always special. Even if some of the family members did not come, we always had a feast. The first course consisted of spaghetti with the most delicious tomato sauce, followed by a large platter of delicate veal cutlets overlapping down the middle of the serving dish, with small potato balls browned at either end, and peas and carrots. A salad was next with cheese and then Marcel would outdo himself with a dessert— souffles, "Floating Island," mousses, cakes, ices, on and on—always delicious.

It was Auntie's daily job to go over the menu. Marcel would make up menus for several days at a time and send them up with Esther to Auntie. Auntie would either approve, or make suggestions. Marcel did all the marketing at the big marketplace in Washington. I am afraid that this is where he showed some weakness. Uncle gave Marcel a certain amount of money to buy food and Marcel would pad the bills and pocket the difference. In France, this was done all the time, but when Uncle eventually caught on, he had a terrible fight with Marcel. I am sure the butlers were doing the same thing with the Magruder's bill, for on the first of the month, when Uncle would open the bills, he would go into a rage in his third floor office. Uncle would ring for each servant, one at a time, and fire them all. One hour later, he would rehire them. We all were used to this terrible time of the month.

One month, I was involved in this dreadful ordeal. I had received a Kodak camera for my birthday, but no money to buy film. I discovered that the Blairs had a charge account at the Rexall pharmacy on Pennsylvania Avenue. I bought roll after roll of film and took pictures of everything. The film alone was $60.00 one month, which was a lot of money then. I had never seen Uncle so angry. He ranted and raged for 10 minutes, then called for Esther and told her to keep an eye on me and that I was never, never to charge anything again. I wasn't on an allowance then, so this rule made it hard. I would have to ask for everything I needed and Esther would have to go and wheedle it out of him. Esther fought with Uncle to get him to give me more clothes and accessories. Finally, she managed to convince Uncle I needed an allowance. Uncle agreed and gave me one dollar every Saturday morning. The stipulation he attached was that I had to show him how I had spent every cent. He would then show me how extravagant I was, but I felt that if I stayed within my limits, I should be able to spend as I chose without accounting for the money or discussing it.

Although Uncle provided well for all of us, he was a rather stingy person with cash. I have no idea what his income was then, but I do know it cost him $4,000 per month to run Blair House. The servants were getting very low wages—around $123 per month. Seldom was there a raise offered, but they got their bed and board. Some even had their clothes provided. The upstairs maid wore a gray dress with a white apron. The kitchen maid was given a striped dress with an apron. Marcel, the chef, had a white apron and high hat. Vickie and Esther and Madame Jeanne wore their own clothes but were given aprons to protect their dresses.

The servants my Uncle and Auntie really dressed up were the butlers and the chauffeur. The head butler always wore black tails with striped trousers, a stiff wing collar, and a white shirt. The second man had to have the classic usher's outfit of blue trousers and tails with lots of gold buttons and braid. The chauffeur wore dark gray jodhpurs with black boots and a dark gray coat, a white shirt, and a cap. All outfitted servants had at least two changes of clothes given to them each year.

My Sunday chore was being in charge of the grandfather clocks. When I first arrived, I watched Uncle carefully wind up each clock on each landing. I was much too small to reach the face of the clocks, but later on I was allowed to stand on a stool and wind them up and start the pendulum. Eventually that became my job.

Like today, the Sunday papers were enormous. They arrived while we were at church, so all afternoon Auntie and Uncle would read the papers while I tried to amuse myself on the fourth floor. Sometimes Esther would take me out to Madame Jeanne's house for the afternoon, where I could rollerskate around the block. It was always a pleasant diversion to be with Madame Jeanne and her husband, Rene, and their two little boys. Rene was a chef at the French Embassy and so I always had the best Sunday suppers there. Esther and Jeanne were so close that when they had pictures taken, which was frequently, they looked like twins. They even combed their hair the same and, being in the '20s, they dressed a lot alike and wore the same hats. Because of this close friendship, Jeanne's husband, Rene Girault, was a personal friend of Marcel Berthaught, our chef. The four of them planned their life together. I adored Madame Jeanne's little boy, Abel, and would play with him every chance I had.

Blair House often seemed awfully empty to me, especially on weekends and mid-afternoons. I yearned for a pet. I am not sure where we got him from, but suddenly we had a cat. Auntie thought it was a "she" and named her Minette. Then we learned it was a male and renamed it Billy Minette. Billy Minette was a magnificent coon-type cat with a bushy tail and a lovely thick coat. He also ran the roost. He sat on all the precious chairs, especially the needlepoint ones. Poor Auntie had to put towels on all the chairs. He sharpened his claws on most of the sofas and in general drove the butlers wild. Auntie put a collar with bells on Minette to scare the birds away as he stalked them. He managed to learn to stalk without tinkling a single bell, as I learned when I ran into Minette on the fourth floor with a large robin in his mouth. He was indeed a very naughty cat, but loved by all, so he lived on with us in Washington as well as Bar Harbor.

A German Shepherd puppy was the next addition to our household, but he was such a handful that he was relegated to the basement in the care of Marcel and Esther. We named him Rex. He was a beautiful animal and fairly well trained, considering he never went to obedience school. Uncle liked him because he thought it gave the house some protection, but the only person he ever bit was me! I was about 16 at the time and Rex was aging. I was stroking his muzzle and was readily warned by his growls to lay off, but I didn't, and suddenly he turned on me and sank his teeth into my right arm. That caused a major crisis. A doctor was called; the wound had to be cauterized, and it took weeks to heal. Uncle wanted the dog put down immediately, but many tears later he was spared and lived on another five years.

My eighth year was one full of action. This was the year that I decided to step out of my fourth floor bedroom window onto the ledge and walk along until I arrived at the joining house, Blair Lee House, and look in the dormer windows to the room that belonged to Vickie Geaney and her family. I had such fun doing this that I repeated the same performance several mornings in a row around 6:00 a.m. The guard across the street at the White House gates finally spied an apparition in night clothes walking along the ledge. He must have thought the Blairs had some insane person locked up in the attic. He was so upset that he came across the Avenue and rang the doorbell. He must have had a long wait, as no one was around at that time of day. Eventually the butler who lived in the basement answered the door. What a shock he must have had to hear the guard ask if there was some mentally ill person upstairs walking along the ledge! By that time, I was back in my room in bed. It wasn't until a day or two later that Uncle questioned me. I had to admit doing it, as I had startled Vickie out of her wits' end by knocking on her window next door. Wooden bars were put on all the fourth floor windows but they were useless, as I pointed out to the family, as all I had to do was to loosen them and climb out again. Even though I promised not to repeat the same performance, they didn't trust me and replaced the wooden bars with an accordion gate, which was to be locked in place each night. That was worse, as I was mortified and felt like a caged animal. I think the Blairs were beginning to think I was becoming a handful.

Although I didn't really enjoy playing with dolls, I did enjoy the dollhouse that arrived one Christmas. The house was electrified, which made it very special at night. It was very large and contained many rooms, and had lots of furniture. I enjoyed moving the furniture around and adding more to each room, but I did not have any small people living in this house. What I did have living in this mansion was my pet Easter duck. He was just a baby and all yellow and fluffy. He would follow me down the hall and all around the house. I poured a lot of love on this little duckling. I filled the bathtub with water and let him walk up and down the stairs of the dollhouse. He loved it, but of course made a terrible mess. I would hear him every morning calling to me from the playroom. One morning, he didn't call me and I tore in there only to find him dead. It was a terribly sad day for me. He was buried in a shoe box in the garden, with the butler Alfred officiating at the service. All my pets were buried in the garden, including a box turtle, a frog, and several birds, along with the painted turtles from the five and ten.

One of my very early friends was Josephine Boyle, who lived in the Mayflower Hotel with her grandfather, Judge McCoy. She often would come down to the house and play with me all afternoon. One of the outstanding things we did was to sled down the steps from the top floor to the first floor, banging to a terrible halt at each landing. I hate to think what it did to the stair carpets, but since no one was watching over us we had a ball. Esther finally came home and caught us in the act, but I doubt if the Blairs ever found out. The house had an Otis elevator, which went from the basement to the fourth floor. As youngsters we would ride endlessly up and down until someone called it to a halt. Auntie and Uncle always went out driving around in the afternoons, which gave me free reign for a couple of hours to get into all kinds of trouble.

Madame Jeanne was rarely there on weekends and always left by five or six o'clock during the week. She taught me French grammar and reading and French conversation, along with manners and how to dress properly and how to eat. She was a wonderful person and I loved her and Esther dearly. Auntie was much too busy with her social life to fool around with me. It was Uncle who took a special interest in everything I did. We loved to play hide-and-seek late in the afternoon. For a man going on 70, he was most patient with me. I used to love to sit on the edge of his sleigh bed and slide down backwards and do somersaults. He never reprimanded me for this kind of play as I watched him dress for dinner. I would help with his coat and tie, tuck his watch and chain in the appropriate pockets, put his glasses on his nose, tie his shoes, and brush off his clothes just like Robert did in the morning. Uncle was a firm believer that one should always change one's clothes or at least one's shoes before dinner.

Top: Aunt Laura Blair as a bride to first husband Franklin H. Ellis
Bottom: Aunt Laura Blair

Top: Gist Blair in 1904 with the Chevy Chase Club Horseshow Committee. Seated from left to right: Alexander B. Legare, Reginald S. Huidekoper, Hubert G. Dering, Walter D. Denegre, Frederic L. Huidekoper. Standing: Woodbury Blair, Nathaniel S. Simpkins, Gist Blair, Clarence Moore.

Bottom: Laura feeding pigeons in Lafayette Square, aged 7 (1929-1930)

Top: Henri de Charmont, our French chauffeur (circa 1938).

Bottom: Esther Ekberg, Aunt Laura's Personal assistant.

Top: Marcel, our chef, Bar Harbor, ME.

Bottom: Uncle Gist at Deauville, France (1923).

Top: *John, The gardener, at Bar Harbor, ME, Cousin Dorothy Wyeth, and Uncle Gist*

Bottom: *Esther, Madame Jeanne (my governess), and her child, Abel.*

Top: (From left to right) Laura, Madame Staub (my governess), Pulitzers' governess, and Michael and Elinor Pulitzer at Bar Harbor, ME.

Bottom: Mary, our kitchen maid, Laura, and Esther at Sandy Beach, Bar Harbor, ME.

Top: Pulitzers' governess, Madame Staub, Elinor Pulitzer, and Laura at Bar Harbor, ME.

Bottom: Pulitzer staff member, Laura, Esther, and Marcel at Jordan Pond, Seal Harbor, ME.

Top: Complete staff of Pulitzer and Blair household at dock in Bar Harbor, ME.

Bottom: Laura's 10th birthday at Blair House (Easter Day).

Top: Franklin Ellis, Bob Lawson, Kate Ellis, and their son, Henry.

Bottom: Henry Ellis and Bob Lawson at Dupont Circle, Washington, D.C.

CHAPTER VII.

Relatives

Aunt Laura had a sister whom I called Aunt Nanna. She was quite a character, to say the least. She was married to Uncle Walter Wilcox, who was a prominent amateur photographer and one of the first people to visit Lake Louise and capture that beautiful sight on film. He also did portrait sittings, disappearing behind his black cloth. They never had any children. They spent their time visiting abroad and socializing. They lived at 1526 New Hampshire Avenue, where they frequently entertained at lavish parties. The home is now the headquarters for the Women's National Democratic Club.

Since Auntie was her only sister, Nanna frequented Blair House and was usually at Sunday lunches. She always brought her little wretched Pekinese, a real lapdog and one that never seemed to miss having an accident on the rug under the dining room table. This caused a dilemma, as the butlers had to race around cleaning up the messes. The Peke would never eat like a normal dog, but she would eat in Aunt Nanna's lap, making a bigger mess. We used to hate it when she came with her Peke. However, to make up for this, Aunt Nanna was amusing, as she was most eccentric, especially when she grew older. She had, late in life, dyed her hair red. She wore too much powder and clothes that should have gone to the cleaners months before and she chain-smoked. She had been quite a belle in her earlier years, but after the crash of '29, she and Uncle Walter lost everything.

I suppose Uncle considered them another set of Auntie's poor relations. Uncle Walter gradually faded out of the picture and lived at the Chevy Chase Club, where he died in 1949, a year before Nanna. I remember visiting Aunt Nanna in New York in a small flat. Everything was always so seedy. She must have been an embarrassment to Auntie. Uncle very generously allowed her to visit us in Bar Harbor each summer for a month or so. Unfortunately, she had become a heavy drinker by this time and so half the time she was tipsy or reeked of vodka. No one knew quite what to do with her. Her silly sense of humor kept her welcome, but not without a groan or two. Uncle had purchased the large house next to "Cleftstone" called "Hillhurst" to accommodate all the relatives who liked to summer in Bar Harbor. They had their own maids and kept house, but Uncle wanted a complete accounting of every nickel spent on food and other necessities. Cousin Dorothy was in charge of record keeping.

Cousin Dorothy Wyeth, daughter of Auntie's brother William C. Lawson, was born in Cincinnati and grew up in Cleveland. She visited Aunt Laura at Blair House many times in her youth and eventually met her future husband at Blair House. They were married in 1919. Her husband, Nathan Wyeth, was a famous architect and designed many important buildings in Washington, including the Embassies of Russia, Mexico, Afghanistan, Morocco, and Chile. He also was the architect of the National Guard Armory, the Municipal Center, Georgetown Library, the Woodrow Wilson and Thomas Jefferson Schools, the Tidal Basin Bridge, the Columbia and Emergency Hospitals, and the old Lemon Building on New York Avenue. The Lemon Building is now part of the headquarters of the American Institute of Architects, which also owns the Octagon House next door. He designed this building in 1891 and personally helped to construct it. The beautiful library in Blair House was also one of Cousin Nathan's works.

Although Cousin Dorothy was only 19 when she met the much older and shy architect, Nathan, they had a bond through France, where they had both studied. Cousin Nathan spent 10 years at Ecole des Beaux Arts in Paris after graduating from the Art School of New York City's Metropolitan Museum of Art. Cousin Dorothy had spent most of her teen years in France. On this bond they built a life which revolved around his career, her vigorous social life, and a shared zest for sports and the outdoors. She was an excellent tennis player and won many tournaments. A favorite activity during their trips to Europe was climbing in the Alps. During the war and beyond the age for conscription, Cousin Nathan worked in the Army's construction division, taking a Major's pay. He loved France and at that point France was in a bad way. His intelligence was his gift to France. He worked very hard and lost his health, so he spent several years recuperating in Switzerland. When he returned, he had to start over again on his career. It took him six years to get his practice back. Just as he was going "great guns" with embassy and private commissions, the stock market crashed. Because of these financial difficulties and after 12 years as a municipal architect, he finally retired. Cousin Dorothy went out in the world and became a social secretary. She rotated between the French and the Brazilian Embassies, arranging all of their parties and paying heed to protocol. Cousin Dorothy was special. She did such a grand job for the different ambassadors and their wives with their tight social life that they decided to honor her.

Cousin Dorothy received the Legion of Honor at the French Embassy in 1952. She wore a chic black tissue-taffeta dress accented with velvet and pearls. On her head she wore a garland of deep pink posies. Mme. Bonnét, rushing up to offer her congratulations, wore a Paris product of black silk encrusted with braid. A large reception of her family and close friends followed this presentation.

Besides making a nice living being a social secretary, Cousin Dorothy became head of the American Men's Voluntary Services. In this spot she had charge of information, registration, files, forms, typists, mimeographing, the victory booths, and repairs for the building. When I was older and our country was at war, she soon put me to work as well as a nurse's aid at the Emergency Hospital.

Uncle loved Cousin Dorothy and often asked her advice as to whether he was rearing me correctly. She was critical of me but I loved her. She arranged a lot of my early birthday parties and saw to it that I was entered in Miss Hawk's dancing school for boys and girls. She helped Auntie pick out my clothes and lectured me on etiquette, manners, and morals. She always smoked with a holder and played bridge brilliantly. She was a natural at bringing together Washington's most elite group at different functions. Her handwriting was perfect, as she addressed hundreds of invitations. Her visits to Blair House were numerous and ones I looked forward to with great excitement.

Dorothy and Nathan had two good-looking children, Margo and Stuart. Margo's wedding was one of the big functions of my growing-up years. It was all so exciting and so beautiful that I wanted to be a bride, too. Her son, Stuart, while still at Harvard, would come to the house occasionally. He was tall, good-looking, and most charming. I must have had a crush on him, for I wished that I were older. He married Caroline Levering and had five children. Margo married Herbert Statford, manager of "Morton Salt," and moved to Chicago, so I never saw much of her until much later on. Cousin Nathan lived on into his 90s but didn't want to leave the apartment, so Cousin Dorothy lived her own life, returning home only in the evenings. On one anniversary, a good friend of theirs quoted the following: "Nathan's courts and schools remind us Man can build to heights divine. And departing, leave behind us blueprints on the sands of time. In the poetic words of Montgomery Blair, 'Drink hearty and give the house a good name.'"

Other family members who had a tremendous impact on my life were Ginney and Monty Blair. Monty, a pediatrician and my doctor, was Uncle's favorite nephew. He was probably closer to Uncle than any of the other surviving Blairs at the time. Uncle's brother Woody had died and Uncle transferred his affection to Monty. His wife, Ginney, was another "brick." They had four lovely girls, with whom I played all during my growing-up years. Ginney was another administrator. She was the head of Junior League and Planned Parenthood, served on one board after another, and still managed to raise her daughters. Monty and Ginney loved to play golf at Chevy Chase and bridge in the evenings. For years, they attended St. John's Church, but later joined Christ Episcopal Church in Georgetown.

Ginney had been born in Washington and graduated from the old Western High School. She attended the Convent de Dames Anglaise in Belgium. She later was a vice chairman of D.C. Citizens for Eisenhower and was co-chairman of the President's Inaugural Celebration. Ginney became more and more part of my life as I grew older, but in the early days it was Monty whom I saw the most. He came to my bedside when I had measles, flu, or colds. He always was so kind and made me feel ever so much better before his departure even though his visits sometimes meant an enema, which was the cure-all in the '20s.

Uncle always had it in his mind to leave the house to Monty upon his death. He would have Monty stop by on many occasions to talk about the future. There was always the threat of the Government buying the property and tearing down all the lovely houses for office buildings. Later, when I was around 17, this threat almost became a reality during Franklin Roosevelt's presidency. Uncle invited the President to come over for a visit and discuss the entire plan. Roosevelt was so impressed with the lovely 19th century house and all the beautiful furnishings that he promised Uncle that as long as he was in office he would see to it that nothing would happen to Blair House. At a later date, some of the block was demolished for office space, but at least the Pennsylvania Avenue side and Jackson Square have remained intact. Uncle would sit down with Monty and make "definite plans." However, when the time did come in 1942, Ginney and Monty were very happy living on Kalorama Circle and did not wish to move to Blair House. Thus, Percy Blair, then with the State Department, pressed for a decision to buy the house for use as the official guest house of the United States Government. This probably saved the entire block from becoming another series of tall buildings.

Monty had graduated from Princeton University in 1922, the year I was born, and earned a medical degree from Harvard Medical School in 1925. He interned for two years at St. Luke's Hospital in New York and finally came to Washington as an intern at Children's Hospital. For 12 years, beginning in 1930, he was a pediatrician here. He served in the Army Medical Corps during World War II and joined Children's Hospital as a director in 1947. He was devoted to his cause and later he oversaw the building that opened in 1952, which contained a nursery for infants in critical condition and additional patient beds. He also became chairman of the Red Cross Blood Bank and the Regional Blood Center.

Monty was a tall, good-looking man with a very gentle side to him, most of the time. I only remember once that he lost his temper with me, and that was in Bar Harbor. I was 14 at the time and had just gotten my driver's license and couldn't wait to drive everything and anything I could get my hands on. They owned a little black Ford, which Ginney always allowed me to drive when they weren't using it. One day, they asked me to drive them over to the golf club, and, according to Monty, I was to leave the car at the club for them so as to have a ride home, but I understood him to say that I was to leave the car at home as they would get a ride with someone else. Around five o'clock that afternoon, I saw them staggering down Cleftstone Road carrying all their clubs over their shoulders. I ran and greeted them, so proud that I had left the car just as I thought I was told to do, when the blast came. I had never seen anyone so angry in all my life. Even Uncle never got that angry. Cousin Monty called me everything in the book—inconsiderate, selfish, disobedient, etc., etc. I was crushed! I cried and cried, especially since I thought I had done nothing wrong. It took days before I was even allowed in the house to see him. Finally, Ginney smoothed things over and I was allowed to come and apologize. I was never allowed to drive the car again. His daughters used to tell me years later that I softened him for them so that they were able to get away with a bit more without suffering his temper. I always loved being around them from my early years on. They were always wonderful to me, and we soon forgot that dreadful day in Maine.

Auntie's only son, Franklin Ellis, was another frequent visitor to Blair House, but mostly only to visit his mother and to secure a check from her if possible, as he was always in need. I don't think Uncle had too much in common with him. Franklin was very matter-of-fact, rather dull and boring and would go on and on pressing some point that no one was the least bit interested in. He was a very curious person and would embarrass everyone by asking extremely personal questions. He did have two lovely sons, Henry and Garry. They were always a lot of fun, which made up for the dull visits Cousin Franklin would provoke. Franklin remarried a tiny person called Helen, who seemed to be very happy with him. When they had any disagreements, Helen would stay in her room for days without any meals. She would always win her point in this fashion and all would be well for a while. They loved to motor and would do so all up and down the East Coast, visiting people along the way. When I went to see Franklin in 1960 as he was dying of cancer, he still had the curiosity to ask me whom I was living with, as he knew I was divorced at the time. He always got people to satisfy his insatiable curiosity. I think most people were so taken by surprise that they couldn't think of an evasive answer.

When Auntie and Uncle were still well and young enough to entertain, they had lovely dinner parties. I was supposed to be in bed, but I couldn't help sneaking down to the pantry to watch the butlers come and go with the different courses. Getting ready for such a party took days of preparation. Auntie would come down and pick out the lace table cloth, the china, the glass, and the silver. There would always be a different combination, as the Blairs had plenty of beautiful china, silver, and crystal.

After this was done, Auntie would ring for Marcel to decide on the menu. Instead of always using the silver serving dishes, she would have Marcel make beautiful baskets out of peanut brittle in which "les petites pois vert" would be served. He also made small baskets with handles for the carrots. I would often watch Marcel make these baskets, which took several days as they had to cool and be shaped many times before they were ready.

A typical menu in these years was:

Consommè Royale
Crepes farcies
au crabe
Selle d'Angeau rôtie
Salade
Glace aux marrons

Among some of their guests would be Mrs. William Howard Taft, the Warren Barbours, the Sumner Wells, the Breckinridge Longs, the Peter Jays, Mrs. Woodbury Blair, the Marshall Langhornes, the Nelson Perins, Mrs. Cary Langhorne, Mrs. Edward Mitchell, the Richard Wilmers, Mrs. Kent Legare, the Hamilton Fishes, the Nathan Wyeths, Princess Boncompagni, the John Newbolds, the DeForest Grants, Clarence Stetson, the John Dorrances, the James Clement Dunns, the Chatfield-Taylors, the Charles Glovers, Harold Ikes, Justice Holmes, Mr. and Mrs. Cordell Hull, Mrs. Truxton Beale, the Reginald Huidekopers, and many others of the national society. Most of the dinner parties were for around 20 guests, but other parties were smaller.

Once everything was all set up, they would have a series of dinner parties. Auntie was a wonderful housekeeper and arranged all the flowers herself. She always saw to it that there were chocolate mints on the dining room table. The gentlemen went upstairs to the library after dinner and the ladies retired to the front parlor. Coffee, liqueurs, and cigarettes would be passed to the ladies and the gentlemen would light up good cigars in the library and a very rare port would be poured. The gentlemen entered the downstairs parlor after a long discussion on politics and foreign affairs. In my early years at Blair House, quite a lot of the after-dinner conversation dwelled upon Europe and what was Hitler really going to do and would we eventually get sucked into another war. No one, apparently, really thought that this would happen, nor did they think that Hitler was a threat to anyone. If Uncle had lived a bit longer, he would have been shocked at the course of events.

Peering down from my perch on the first landing, I could see all the guests being given their coats and hats, laughing and bidding each other a pleasant night. Uncle always did the locking up himself, even though it was the butler's job to check all the windows and doors. At this point I would run quickly up the back steps to my room on the fourth floor and pretend to be asleep.

Uncle always came up to listen outside my door to see if I was asleep. He rarely opened the door—I could have been watching a movie at the "Earle." He seemed so sure I was safely in bed.

CHAPTER VIII.

A Year Abroad

Around 1932, it was planned that Blair House would be rented to friends and we would spend a whole year abroad. Auntie was getting much more feeble with her Parkinson's, but still was able to get around. It took Esther much longer now to dress her and curl her hair, as her head was getting more and more bent over. Also, Auntie's hands were shaking terribly. I used to feel so sorry for her and would often sit with her and help her in and out of chairs. I believe Uncle thought the trip to Europe would distract her mind from her health.

We spent a month at the Hay-Adams House around the corner before departing from New York on the "Washington." Being 10, I was much more conscious of all the details of this trip. Trunks were brought down from the attic and I had never seen so many clothes as Esther packed in these wardrobe trunks. My trunk was the same old one that I had been using since I was five. Esther had to take charge of this, as I would not have known what to pack. Right before the trip, I was off on many shopping excursions with Auntie and Esther, since I was outgrowing everything.

The staff was to stay on at Blair House and be with the people who were renting. Only Esther accompanied us to Cannes, where we were to spend the winter at the Grand Hotel on the Croisette. We were seen off by the entire Blair House staff and some of Auntie and Uncle's special friends and family. I remember the excitement of arriving at the pier, being shown to our cabins, and the shouting and waving as the whistle blew as we set off. My cabin was an inside one again, but being older I didn't mind it. I had an early Westclock with numerals you could see in the dark. It was my friend, and I would rely on this clock to tell me when it was morning.

I enjoyed all of the activities on board and joined Uncle in his horse racing, which is the one thing he liked to gamble on. He would let me pick the horse and he would put a dollar on it. We seldom won, but we never gave up. Shuffleboard was another one of his interests, which even Auntie could play with the help of Esther. The rest of the time we would just walk up and down the decks or all the way around the ship. I used to look forward to the mid-morning bouillon with crackers and lounging on the deck chairs, watching the sea birds dive for the garbage that the ship would toss in the ocean from time to time. I also played quoits and badminton with shipboard peers and attended children's movies every afternoon. I also enjoyed Punch and Judy shows. There was so much to do, including eating three wonderful meals a day.

Auntie and Uncle had made some friends and were soon involved with nightly bridge games and cocktail parties before dinner. We didn't always eat together. I sometimes would eat with Esther and some friends of hers, but most of the time we all ate as a family. If it became the least bit rough, Auntie would stay below, as she was becoming very unsteady on her feet. On the next to last day, we sailed past the Rock of Gibraltar, which I had learned a bit about in school, and I was excited to really see it. Esther showed me the coast of Spain with all the tile roofs, and the little coastal villages. We docked at Marseilles, as Uncle had ordered a car and chauffeur to meet us and drive us to Cannes.

Arriving at the hotel in Cannes was quite a performance. Uncle would count the suitcases a dozen times a day even before we were ready to leave the ship. We had so many, many different bags—Auntie alone had hat boxes, shoe cases, and small, large, and huge valises. There was also hand luggage for me, Uncle, and Esther. This didn't even count the wardrobe trunks, which were sent over by express several days later. I guess being away for a whole year did mean a lot of clothes for many different seasons, as Cannes can be quite hot, Vevey cool, and Paris rainy and damp.

The Grand Hotel, which has since been torn down, was a magnificent structure. A long double driveway lined with palms and palmettos and flowers led up to the gracious front door with a canopy. The large windows on either side of the front door had sort of balloon awning with white fringe. It was indeed an elegant hotel. The concierge met us at the door to greet our arrival and several "grooms d'hotel" helped us with our many bags. We had a suite overlooking the Croisette and the Mediterranean Sea. We had a handsomely appointed living room with Louis XV French furniture and lots of ormolu on the desk and marble top tables. Auntie and Uncle had separate bedrooms with baths and I had a double room shared with Esther with our own bath. I had never seen beds made up with bolsters. Chambermaids came in frequently to check on things and bring fresh towels twice a day. It was all so new to me and so thrilling. I couldn't wait to explore the outdoors—especially the beach.

It wasn't long before I was trusted to play on the beach without Esther watching over me, as I had promised not to go near the water. I especially liked a springboard that I could run up to, take a huge jump, and sail through the air to land on the soft sand. There was also a large rubber ball that I could stand on and try to roll it along the sand without falling off. Building sand castles with trenches and moats kept me busy by the hour. I never saw Uncle venture near the beach. I would rather imagine he would have been a sight to behold in a bathing suit with his long skinny legs and pot belly. In the gardens of the hotel was an enclosed golf practice with a pro called "Tino Trastour," who was young, handsome, and very patient as a teacher. He soon made friends with Esther and they became inseparable. Esther seemed to have a lot of charm with the opposite sex. Marcel was totally forgotten for the time being. Tino was around a lot and I, as a young girl approaching 11, was enamored with him. He used to call me "Mon petit bebe rose."

Cannes, being a fishing town of old, was charming with cobbled streets and quaint shops—the Patisserie Shops were my favorites! Seldom could Esther and I pass one without indulging in their gateaux, les tourteaux, and les tablettes de chocolates. Esther used to love to take me way up a steep hill to visit an ancient church at the very top overlooking the whole city and the sea. At sunset this was especially beautiful. Esther taught me to light a candle and say a prayer. Sometimes when we visited this church we would remain kneeling for a long time. The stained glass windows were always reflecting different lights, depending on the time of day. Sometimes I saw a golden hue right on the altar enveloping the Cross with Jesus upon it. I would weep for Him and His suffering. I used to stare at His face and wonder what it would have been like to have known Him as a person. "Why did He only come once?" I thought. "Why couldn't He come again so I could see Him?" It all seemed so unfair. These were my thoughts as I sat on the hard wooden benches with Esther. On the way home, we would wander through the streets of Cannes and marvel at all the decorated windows, for Christmas was coming soon. Street vendors sold hot biscuits, French bread, and les petits pains. It seemed so romantic to me. I wanted to stay in Cannes forever.

Soon after we arrived and settled into our new quarters at the hotel, Uncle enrolled me in a little French American school called "Cours Maintenon." We all wore little blue smocks over our regular clothes. Our hired chauffeur drove me to school each morning and came to fetch me in the afternoon. Classes started at eight o'clock and I was home by four. It seemed a long day to me, as I had to accustom myself to a completely different way of life. Although there were four or five American children in my class, the majority were all French girls and much further along in their education than was I. The desks were all attached together. One long bench accommodated us all in each row and to move in or backwards, everyone would have to stand up and pull together. We stayed in one room most of the day. We had to learn all the provinces of France (which to me seemed endless), and learn to spell them correctly and to find them on the map.

The daily dictée would come next, which would throw me for a loop, as I didn't seem to know how to spell anything. A nice little French girl on my left often let me copy off of her dictée book, which kept me from being "numero zero" in the class each week. Arithmetic was way beyond me. The rest already understood algebra and fractions. I could hardly do the long division or fractions. I was so embarrassed to be such a dumb bunny! It took me months to catch up and catch on. I was last in the class every single week until Uncle asked what in tarnation I was doing at this school. I tried to explain to him that I was working as hard as I knew how, but I just couldn't catch up with the others. I was so unhappy and told my little French classmates of my plight. They felt so sorry for me that they all pitched in to help me learn and hand in better papers. I cheated with their help, and soon I was at the head of the class. Uncle was so pleased. I couldn't keep up this pace for long, especially since the teacher caught on that I was copying. I was isolated and my grades soon fell back to zero again. It took five months for me to finally struggle up to sixth in my class and there is where I stayed for the balance of the year. I believe in retrospect that I learned a more valuable lesson for life in the kindness of my little French friends than I would have learned at the school had I been able to do all the work on my own.

We students all stayed at the school for lunch, followed by recess in an enclosed yard, which unfortunately had no swings or other playground equipment. We played hopscotch and tag. The afternoon classes were as hard as the morning French lessons. We had to learn English history— including the dates for all the kings and queens. Reading and writing were easier, but the daily demands were such that I wonder to this day why I didn't develop an ulcer.

I stayed well most of the winter despite a real snow in January, when Cannes became extremely cold and all beach fun was out. Uncle and Auntie had to abandon their walks and I was relegated to finding fun in the hotel lounges until spring.

I had learned all the Aesop fables in French and would amuse the family and other guests of the hotel by reciting them in the evening and acting out the parts as well. There was a little stage in one of the dance halls and I would stand up there all alone without being the least bit shy. Auntie and Uncle would clap and I would make a little curtsy and recite fable after fable.

It was spring when I came down with chicken pox and simultaneously Uncle came down with shingles—the two apparently go hand in hand. Uncle's shingles were in his head and affected his eyes so that he couldn't read. He suffered enormous pain. Esther made compresses for him dipped in some solution which smelled like a disinfectant. It didn't really do any medical good, but perhaps it helped sooth the blisters and the pain.

It was no wonder Uncle came down with shingles considering what was going on back home. Franklin D. Roosevelt was the president-elect, obliged to wait four months before taking office. The Inauguration would not take place until March 4, 1933. During this long interregnum, Roosevelt had to sit on the sidelines while the country's economy edged toward complete chaos. Thousands of banks closed their doors to forestall a run on their dwindling liquid assets by anxious depositors and some never opened again. Roosevelt refused to share responsibility with the "Lame Duck" occupant of the White House. It would all have to wait until after March 4. I heard long discussions between Uncle and his business associates and I am sure he was scared to death as to what would become of his assets. He must have transferred a lot of money into the French banks to cover our expenses over there, but what about back home? Perhaps it was the worry that finally brought on the worst case of shingles the doctor had ever seen. Everything seemed to come to a stop for a few weeks. Esther was seldom seen except hovering over Uncle's head or taking care of Auntie. I remained in bed with my chicken pox for several weeks before returning to school.

Near the end of the semester, warm weather came back again and I was allowed to play on the beach. The family discussed summer plans—we were to leave Cannes after school was over and spend the summer in Vevey, Switzerland. I had made some friends by this time. The Kelley sisters and Patricia Burton from New York were my playmates, as they also lived in the Grand Hotel. I hated the thought of leaving them and my beloved Cannes, which I adored.

As the move approached, I announced that I had been having a pain in my side for several days. The doctor decided that I should be operated on in an American hospital just north in the hills behind Cannes. Off I went to the hospital with Uncle and Esther in the ambulance with me. I had wonderful nurses and a beautiful private room but I was miserable. For two long weeks, I lay in bed suffering from pain and feeling weak all over. I think Uncle thought I was probably going to die. He never left my side until I began to feel better and could get up and walk around a bit. When I was discharged, I was carried on a stretcher to the ambulance and delivered to the hotel.

As soon as it was prudent to leave, Esther packed us up again and we prepared to drive to Vevey. The police arrived just as we were leaving and stopped our trunks from being picked up. We had made a mistake about duty taxes. Uncle was furious for the delay and also he must have felt that there was no cause to pay any more duty on his trunks, so he promptly lost his temper and threatened to have the poor man fired if he didn't lift the ban immediately. I think this Agent de Police was so intimidated that they let us go.

I didn't see much of the Swiss scenery or the simple but lovely hotel in which we stayed for some weeks to come, as I slept almost continuously due to the altitude and my weakened condition. It was all Esther could do to get me up for meals. I even fell asleep at the table. The family didn't seem too upset—maybe someone reassured them that it was perfectly normal for a recuperating 11-year-old to sleep for several weeks. One day I did finally wake up feeling terrific—hungry and full of energy.

The hotel was high above Vevey, with a fantastic view of the Alps and Mont Blanc in the distance. There were farms all around, which delighted me because of my love for chickens, ducks, pigs, etc. I spent a lot of time helping the farmers bring in the hay and feed the livestock.

My only calamity during our stay was the day I rode my little wagon full blast down the winding road that led to the little town of Vevey. I finally fell off and opened both knees. With no brakes, I wonder to this day what I thought I was doing. My knees required stitches and I had a very painful recovery.

Auntie and Uncle and Esther took me on long drives up and down the mountains. We stopped for lunch along the way and bought lots of Swiss candy, hot chocolate, and cheese.

We went to see "Chateau Chillon" one day. What thrilled me was that it had torture chambers. My strong imagination really took off after this visit. I imagined King Arthur and all his knights living in a beautiful chateau like that. I had loved it when Uncle would read all those medieval stories to me. Now, however, Uncle could not read to anyone and before long I was asked to read the front page of the newspaper to him. This task was most trying on my nerves, as I couldn't have cared less at that time of my life about what was going on back home or in Europe. But read I did, and if he liked the headline then I would have to read the rest of the column. I would pray that he would hate the headlines and sometimes I would skip over one that I knew he would want me to read all the rest of. Esther continued with his treatments but Uncle was not getting any better. The pain was subsiding a little but he would have terrible attacks, especially if he got excited about something. His poor bald head was always beet red and very sore.

In the early fall, we were driven to Paris with all our numerous suitcases. The trunks had been shipped ahead of us. We stayed at the Plaza Athenèe on the Avenue Montaigne. It was another exquisite hotel with a well-appointed suite of rooms. Paris held excitement for me, as my best friend from Washington, Josephine Boyle, was also staying in Paris with her mother and grandfather. We met daily, playing on the Champs Élysées, where the merry-go-round operated all the time. The game we played was to ride the horses and try to see how many rings we could spear as we went around. Whoever could spear the most would get free rides. We also had a hoop that we would roll up and down the gravel walkways that lined the Champs Élysées.

The Jardin d'Acclimatation located in the Bois de Boulogne was a park dedicated to newborn or very young animals of all kinds. There were piglets, lambs, puppies, kittens, baby elephants, bear cubs, etc. Upon entering this "jardin," one would buy a bottle or two of milk with nipples and, if lucky, catch one of the wandering babies and feed them their milk. The piglets and the lambs were the most fun, for these I could hold in my lap and pretend that they were my very own. The baby elephants got countless peanuts. The bear cubs were fed their milk without the nipple—it was simply poured right down their throats. The bears were behind wire, but still accessible. Mother bear was in another enclosure. Esther would take Jo and myself to this "jardin" rather frequently.

When Uncle felt a little better, he would walk with me all the way to L'Etoile and back, showing me things of interest.

Auntie and Esther went to the famous couturiers such as Molineux, to pick out fabulous fashions to be brought back to the States. Although Auntie's health was failing, she still desired clothes in fashion and, of course, as far as she was concerned, that was the point of being in Paris. Auntie spent a lot of time and money having dresses made for her in New York, Washington, D.C., or Paris. She was very fashion conscious and always made sure she was dressed in the latest fashions. Until she came down with Parkinson's, she had the "hourglass" figure so praised at the time. She loved to wear dresses that emphasized her sloping shoulders and all her clothes had very tight waists. Lacing her sturdy corsets took the strength of Esther and sometimes me, and even Uncle when Esther wasn't available. Auntie loved lace, lots of embroidery, rosettes, and flowers, silks, and crepes.

For day, she preferred tailored suits made of the finest tweeds, and wool and overcoats with a fur collar. She had a mink coat, of course, as everyone in her status had. Her evening clothes were the most beautiful and the most elaborate. She wore her diamond tiara as often as possible. As a younger woman, she wore her hair piled on top of her head, which gave her a Grecian look, as she had very dark hair and very dark large brown eyes. As an older person, she settled for the popular marcel waves. These were created by using the curling irons heated on little sterno cans.

Auntie's underclothes were as special as the rest of her wardrobe. All of her chemises, underpants, and nightgowns were made in Paris. She had her initials embroidered on each article. All of her underwear had to be sent out to a French laundress, who sent them back all wrapped in pink tissue. Sometimes Esther would gently wash out her chemises and I would have the privilege of ironing them. Esther had taught me how to do this without burning them. Remember the irons were not adjusted to linens, cottons, etc. as they are today. Often we would have to heat the iron and test it on another fabric before daring to use it on the linens or silks. And then we had to use another cloth under the iron just in case something went wrong.

Her shoes were always bought at "Slaters" in Washington. The form never varied—pointed toe, with a strap over the instep. The material, however, ranged from black leather to brown alligator to patent leather to silk in all colors. Her stockings were of silk, of course, as nylon had not appeared as yet. It really took Esther all morning to get Auntie dressed to go out shopping or for luncheon engagements. For a dinner party, Esther would start getting Auntie ready around five in the afternoon.

One of Auntie's favorite pairs of earrings were long pendulums set in diamonds with a large ruby on one ear, an emerald on the other, Port and Starboard arrangement. Her engagement ring, which I now have, is a handsome sapphire set with lots of small diamonds. Uncle had it made for her in Paris. Her wedding band, which matched the platinum of the ring, also came to me and I kept it in my jewelry box. I had been living in Charleston for several years when I suddenly discovered it missing. I was terribly upset at the time and looked everywhere, but to no avail. One day a lady who lived three doors away called me and asked if I knew of anyone with the name of Laura Lawson Blair, as her little dog had been digging in the garden and had found a wedding band with that name. I couldn't believe my good fortune, and quickly explained that it was indeed my aunt's name and the date was her wedding date. Auntie also regularly wore a diamond wristwatch, which came my way upon her death. This met a different fate. In 1970, we had a total house fire with everything burned up except the roof and the standing walls. I had left the watch as usual in my jewelry box. I was sure that all was lost for good. About a week later, after the house had been thoroughly cleaned out and sifted for lost objects, I was standing outside next to the huge pile of rubble, when I happened to look down and there was Auntie's diamond watch in perfect condition with not even a charred mark on it. Now I keep it in the safe deposit box.

Hats were very much in vogue in the 1920s and 1930s and Auntie had her share of them. Some had veils, some did not, some were large, some were small, but all fitted all the way down to the eyes. There were lots of hat shops in Washington on Connecticut Avenue and Esther and Auntie would spend their mornings looking for more hats and shoes.

Auntie wore very little makeup, as Uncle didn't approve of face paint. "Looks cheap," he would say. However, she always wore lots of powder. Esther would dip a large powder puff in loose powder and spread it all over Auntie's face. A trace of light lipstick was added but that was all. I don't think they knew too much about eye makeup, but rouge they did, and Uncle would let Auntie use a little of that. Perfume was always put in atomizers and used liberally.

Uncle's mode of dressing was rather traditional. I always saw him in a three-piece suit made by his tailor in Washington or in London. He favored dark suits in solid blue or a pin stripe. He had one gray suit. He wore white shirts with a stiff wing collar which was the devil to put the collar button in. His ties were also conservative—never a bright red or green. He wore Peal shoes from London, rubbers if there was even a mention of rain, and he always carried either his umbrella or his walking cane. The only time he branched out was in the summer time and in the heat in D.C. when he would wear a navy blue jacket with his waistcoat with white flannel trousers and white shoes. No matter how hot it got, he still wore his long underwear—all one piece.

For golf, Uncle wore knickers, wool socks, and golf shoes of brown and white with a soft white shirt with a jacket. He felt very strongly about changing to a dinner jacket with black patent leather shoes. Later in life, he skipped the dinner jacket and black tie, but would always change his shoes. I used to help him dress in the evening as Robert, the valet, would have left for home. It was fun to stuff his pockets with the appropriate things, such as his watch and gold chain, his silver dollar, his money in a clasp, his wallet, and loose change in another pouch. His pocket contents never changed. He loved bowlers, straw hats, and the regular felt hats. I believe both Auntie and Uncle cut a fine fashion figure at home and abroad.

Our trip home was on the ship called the "Manhattan." It was a very rough crossing and kept most of the passengers in their cabins, unable to face any meals, much less walk about. I kept going, although it was strange to see an empty dining room. Our chef, Marcel, was with us after his visit in Paris and he and Esther joined me. As the storm grew more intense, some of the lounge furniture came loose and slid from side to side, running into the few passengers left on their feet. One poor lady had her leg broken. It became almost impossible to climb the stairs from one deck to the other, as the whole ship seemed to go sideways, then shift to the other side, then buck up and down. It was fun for me but it must have been terrible for the ones who were so ill. Poor Auntie took to her bed and stayed there until the waters became calm again and that wasn't until we were nearly home to New York!

When we were getting ready to dock, we could see a multitude of people waiting to greet everyone. We were greeted by our chauffeur, who helped us with our luggage. The trunks were delivered much later, but we had 15 pieces of hand luggage! Some bags were piled into our car, but most went back to Washington in the butler's car.

CHAPTER IX.

Girlhood 50 Years Ago

Back at the house all was in readiness for us—Vickie had the rugs back down, the heavy draperies back up, and all that tar paper removed from the precious needlepoint chairs. I must say, as lovely as it looked, it did smell strongly of mothballs and tar paper. It was good to be home again, although I had had a wonderful year abroad. I had learned a lot, I loved all the places we went to see, and especially I dreamed of Tino, Esther's friend on whom I had a terrible crush. He was all I could think and dream about at first. He was good-looking and had been so nice to me. I was growing tall and very skinny, but I was slow in developing into a woman. Of course, I was also in love with Gary Cooper and other famous movie actors. I wrote to ask them to send me their autographed photo. They (or their secretaries) did and I had all the photographs framed and hung about my room.

A serious problem concerning school was presented to me. Because of the year I had spent at the Cours Maintenon in Cannes, no one seemed to know just what grade I was supposed to enter. It was finally decided to enroll me in the National Cathedral School for Girls in the Beauvoir section in the sixth grade. I found I was ahead in some things and way behind in others. It was a hard year for me. I had to make new friends, and get used to new teachers and subjects that seemed too hard for me to handle. Only the French class could I tackle right on. The fall passed slowly and I adjusted.

On Christmas day, just before our large dinner, I discovered that I was menstruating for the first time. I had heard all about it from Esther, and I think that for months I had been acting very strange and irritable. Esther would say, "Laura must be getting ready to get her period." I really felt she meant several years hence, but oh no—on Christmas day it appeared. When it was time to descend for lunch and drinks in the lovely front drawing room, I couldn't wait to tell Dr. Monty all about it. I remember running into the room and throwing my arms around his neck and announcing in a loud voice, "Dr. Monty, guess what! Today I am a woman." Slightly taken aback, he asked me what in the world was I talking about. I whispered into his ear and with that, he threw his head back and laughed and laughed. He gave me a gentle hug and told me that I had quite a ways to go yet before I was considered a woman. I groaned to think what Uncle must have thought. He was so protective of me and I had the feeling that from then on I would be watched even more closely, and God help any boys that might come around.

On my twelfth birthday, April 6, the family gave me a lovely birthday party, inviting everyone in my class at school. The dining room was set as though for a banquet, using all the Blairs' best linens, china, and crystal, and the best meal that Marcel could think of just for me. He baked me a three-layer cake as well.

I still had the seventh and eighth grades to master before going away to school at Foxcroft. Miss Templeton was our teacher at Whitby Hall and she was most strict. She taught us American history and English. Miss Addams took care of geography and math. I studied very hard and got good grades, I thought. Little did I realize at the time that my good grades were all a farce. They graded very generously and in fact I wasn't learning much at all, which proved itself when in the eighth grade I was sent down with Cousin Franklin to take my entrance exams for Foxcroft. I apparently knew no Latin or algebra or English grammar. Miss Charlotte sent Uncle a telegram to the fact and suggested that I come another year. Uncle was furious. After much discussion, it was decided that I could come the following fall if I was tutored all summer long up in Bar Harbor. Miss Shiply was interviewed and hired on the spot. I was excited to have someone all to myself and the prospect of going to boarding school sounded terrific to me.

Although Uncle hated to see me go away to boarding school, he felt that it was important for me to get away. I had had a pleasant childhood at Blair House, but had suffered without the companionship of other children and with the great age difference between me and my adoptive parents.

Uncle hoped that if I were constantly surrounded by other girls my own age, I would develop socially. He also wanted to see me become a real lady, prepared to meet the world head-on. He thought a stint at boarding school would correct my social and emotional deficiencies.

I was full of the anticipation of good times, but I was apprehensive as well. I had never been away by myself—not even to camp. I wondered if I would be homesick or not make friends quickly, and I worried that other girls would think I was stupid or make fun of me. I had not been exposed to sophistication as others of my peers had, and I had heard Miss Charlotte of the boarding school remark that I was "a funny little thing." Miss Charlotte had assured Uncle that she would keep her eyes on me and help me mature. I wondered why she thought I was different. I rather think I was so naive and unspoiled, I never thought of myself in need of maturing.

While I was preparing myself psychologically for the trip, Esther prepared my clothes. My uniforms were ordered and Esther sewed my name tapes into all the belongings I would pack.

The bus for Foxcroft left from the railroad station. All of the Washington, D.C. girls piled into the bus and we headed for Foxcroft, which was situated in the foothills of Virginia known as Middleburg. So many of us got car-sick on the way there that the bus driver had to stop several times to let nervous girls out to throw up. The driver had made the trip often and knew what to expect. Usually a girl did not even have to ask to stop. The driver kept a lookout into his mirror and whenever he saw a pale face or a green one, he would automatically stop. The road was a narrow, twisty one, and it seemed to get worse as we neared the school. Finally, we went through the gates and up the hill to Brick House. Miss Charlotte was standing there to greet us. She assigned us to an "old girl" who led us to our quarters, which in those days was called "Porch." "Porch" and "Wing" are now gone, but we had a year and a half before they talked of tearing them down.

The girls were sorted out either two or four to a room, with sleeping accommodations on the screened porch. Iron beds with sleeping bags lined with flannel sheets were used in winter, and incidentally, we were never cold, even though we often woke up with snow on the foot of our beds. Our rooms consisted of a couch, a double bureau, and closets—they were really just a place to keep our things as they were too small and crowded to spend much time in. Communal bathrooms were down the hall.

In almost every room, at least one girl had brought a "Liberty" record player. I had never had a record player back at Blair House, so I didn't know any of the popular songs, let alone sing them. It wasn't long before I realized that there was a lot these girls knew that I did not. They were mostly from New York or Long Island and had lived a much more sophisticated life than I ever knew.

The first few weeks seemed devoted to hazing. We had to braid our hair in a million little braids with ribbons and wear our clothes inside out with our name pinned to our back in large writing. We were told by the older girls that we would have to curtsy or bow in their presence, or sometimes kiss their feet. For one week, the "old girls" were ruthless in their treatment of us, and we new girls lived in fear of them. At the end of the week, we were brought in one at a time in front of the Senior Class and asked all kinds of terrible questions: name all the presidents of the United States, name all the states and their capitals, etc. The worst demand on me was that I sing a song. With no voice at all, I nearly swooned from fear. At last, the dreadful week was over, and we were allowed to be ourselves again.

Our uniforms were rather good-looking—we all wore tan corduroy skirts, but any sweater or blouse was allowed. We each wore a dark green blazer with a fox sewn on the pocket, and brown shoes and socks polished off the image. The style was unfortunately not flattering to all figures and some girls would have looked a lot neater if they had been allowed to wear their own clothes. We all managed a personal touch or two, however. Among the most popular items worn by all the older girls were Brookes sweaters. They were very long cardigans in dark blue, yellow, red, white, etc. I had never seen so stylish a sweater before. All I had were ugly short-sleeved bulky sweaters that pilled all the time. Also, I knew nothing about underarm deodorant, so I went around perspiring too much and my first weeks at school in those hot sweaters I smelled like a polecat. It was the kindness of one of my of classmates that set me straight. She said that, for openers, I should shave under my arms and then use a deodorant. She loaned me hers until I bought my own. No one had ever mentioned shaving, and heaven knows I didn't even know how. All of these little things came out in the open the first few weeks of school.

More personal hygiene came from Miss Emily, our nurse. She would come over in the evening after supper and tell us all about changing our underpants every day. Apparently, some of the girls would wear the same ones for days on end. She told us all about getting our first menstrual period, although most of us had already overcome that hurdle earlier. Miss Emily even gave us a lesson on how to brush our teeth most effectively, and she insisted we wash ourselves daily and wash our hands often. We loved Miss Emily, as she took care of us over at the infirmary when we were sick. She was an all-around good person.

Food played an important role for me in my first weeks at Foxcroft. When I first arrived there, I was declared to be 22 pounds underweight! I had to appear at the infirmary each day for an extra supplement of food and to be weighed. It took me all the way to mid-term to gain all the weight I was supposed to have. It was fun to have milk shakes and candy bars in between meals, while the rest of the girls were only allowed to have fruit.

The dining room in those days was in Brick House. There were several tables, each set for eight and headed by one of the teachers. The middle table was always headed by Miss Charlotte. Miss Eleanor, our riding teacher, Miss Shookie, our athletic director, Miss Emily, and Miss Ayers, the music teacher, each presided at other tables. Girls would fight to sit next to their favorite teacher. A bit of "teacher's pet" came out of all of this and I found I could not compete.

Johnny, the headwaiter, took care of most of the passing of the food, and since we were in Virginia, the cooking was Southern—delicious and plenty of it. Lunch was the main meal, supper was light but sufficient, and tea trays were sent to each house around four-thirty or five. Sticky buns were our favorite food, and homemade brownies our favorite dessert.

71

Miss Charlotte was the heart and soul of Foxcroft and she was very special. She rode beautifully, she was very religious (often preaching to us on Sunday in lieu of our going into town to the little Episcopal Church), and she was strong. She was wonderful with girls. Often she would tell us stories. We listened without a sound. Sometimes Miss Charlotte would gather us all together in the library and read to us. During my four years at Foxcroft, it was Miss Charlotte who was the most instrumental in forming my character. She helped me to be a leader and not always a follower. She picked out the weakness in each girl's makeup and would work on that until the girl showed signs of improvement.

The first trait Miss Charlotte set out to correct in me was my posture. I had to join the posture class several times a week in the gym. I finally got the "Most Improvement in Posture" prize. Miss Charlotte also helped me be a leader by making me a part of "Social Service." I went all over Calhoun County with the head of this service, a nurse who tried to teach the black families how to use birth control. Needless to say, when we would revisit a family six months later, the lady of the house would be six months pregnant. We kept on trying, and sometimes we got through. We issued clothing and all kinds of health aids to the poor. It was a good experience for me, and I am glad that I was exposed to it. Because Miss Charlotte had thought me spineless, I had to work in the very demanding Social Service program a year. She wanted me to learn that when I faced a crisis I shouldn't collapse and cry, but wait until the crisis was solved, and then cry! I carried that piece of advice all my life.

The two competitive groups at Foxcroft were the "Foxes" and the "Hounds." The first day we arrived at Foxcroft, we went to the Fox-Hound room and stood. If anyone in a girl's family had been either a Fox or a Hound, the girl would automatically be in that club. If a girl was the first member of her family to attend Foxcroft, she stood in a circle, and then, going around the circle, every other girl would step into another circle— those in the outer circle were the new Hounds, the inner circle the new Foxes. I became a Hound and dedicated myself to learning to play basketball well enough to beat the Foxes. Miss Charlotte was head of the Foxes and Mrs. Gamble was head of the Hounds. Bitter enemies we became, especially around Thanksgiving time, when the school "Fox Hunt" was held. A large buffet lunch was served on the lawn, followed by the Fox-Hound basketball game.

In order to qualify for the team, one started out her first year on the Cub and Stern teams, gradually working her way up to the School team, and finally as a "sub" on the Fox-Hound team. A really good player would get to play on Thanksgiving Day her last two years, and certainly her senior year. I wanted to be on the team so badly that I even asked Miss Charlotte how to go about it. She suggested that I work with Betsy Babcock, a junior my first year. Betsy agreed to help me, so we went to the gym every minute we could and practiced shooting baskets. Because of this constant practice, I was able to play forward and made the junior team, and finally the Hound team. I had a good eye and could shoot accurately. We beat the Foxes by a large margin my senior year. All of my incentive in basketball was to make up for the fact that I was not turning out to be the super rider that Uncle had anticipated. My basketball ability also gave me a little prestige, which I needed badly.

The honor system was a real tool for development at Foxcroft. If a student talked after hours or during study hall, or smoked or cheated, she was supposed to write down the incident and stick the paper in the honor box. The girl was then punished by being made to trot around the exercise ring (with thumbs up for good posture) as many times as the crime deserved. I was pretty good about reporting myself except for once. I had been falling behind in algebra. In fact, I couldn't understand algebra at all. Uncle was very disappointed in my marks and threatened to pull me out of the school if I didn't work harder and pull my grades up. In the study hall, I was seated just behind one of the smartest girls in my class. It was easy to read over her shoulder and copy her answers to the algebra questions. This helped some of my daily grades, but I still couldn't figure out how she arrived at the answers. Not only did the algebra teacher begin to see through this farce, but an older girl saw me cheat. One day I was taken on a walk after study hall and told I had been seen cheating and that at Foxcroft this was not done. I was so humiliated that I never did anything like that again.

There were two special clubs at Foxcroft. One was known as the "K.K.K." and the other was the "X.M." These clubs were supposed to take in girls who had shown leadership at the school. Selection for the K.K.K. proved to be a heart-breaker for many of us, as we would suddenly see a few of our friends sporting the K.K.K. pins on their jackets. These girls got to help teach primary grades at the local school in the afternoon and on Saturday mornings, and the rest of us felt totally rejected. It was not until my second year was halfway over that I finally received an invitation to join the K.K.K. I probably was the last one, but I didn't care—at least I was in!

After reaching 16, one was eligible for the X.M., which was Miss Charlotte's club, "Understanding Hearts." A single goal was to be a member for life, and to practice having an understanding heart in one's daily life. I was luckier with the X.M. than I had been with the K.K.K., and I received an invitation early in my third year. Each girl was supposed to work on her weakest character point. Mine was defined as being weak, spineless, and not a leader. Miss Charlotte felt very strongly that, if each girl worked on her weakness early in life, it could be corrected. It worked for me, but I do not believe many girls took this seriously. Later in life, when I had serious marital problems, a lot of what I had learned at Foxcroft took me through these bad times.

Another special Foxcroft tradition was the yearly coon hunt. This was particularly fun as we could stay up until midnight as the coon dogs tracked down the coon and finally treed him. We would follow the dogs wherever they went on foot, and finally we would end up back at Brick House for mulligan stew, which was delicious. To this day, I have never mastered the art of cooking mulligan stew to taste as it did at Foxcroft.

Each spring, we were taken on a horseback riding trip to the Luray Caverns. The trip lasted for several days, and girls were only allowed to ride on it if they had kept up their daily riding. We would all start out on a warm May day and ride all morning. The Foxcroft station wagons followed us with all the food and our suitcases. We would stop for lunch along the way, where we would disappear into the woods to relieve ourselves, and then settle down to lamb chops grilled over an open fire. We were allowed a rest of one hour and then we went on until we came to the first night's stop at a large old-fashioned hotel with several beds in each room. The second day, we would take a bus to the Caverns. We spent that night back at our hotel and the next day, we rode back to Foxcroft. We would arrive back at the school tired, dusty, and thirsty, but very happy girls.

These traditions seem so simple now, compared to the schools of today that let the students go wherever almost every weekend. We were only allowed one tea privilege and one weekend away in our third and fourth years. We were content to stay at Foxcroft, however, as we always had fun there together. The only thing we really missed were boys! Boys only sometimes appeared, and then it was just to visit a sister or a friend for an hour or two. The arrival of a boy created a lot of excitement and sometimes one would see a girl with a bit of makeup on.

As my years at Foxcraft progressed, I saw how the girls in my class grew up—and me too! It didn't seem long from our arrival to the time when we were the "old girls" getting ready to graduate. Some girls planned to go on to college and some girls planned their debut.

Going back home for Christmas got more interesting as I grew older and I was allowed to do a little more. I was enrolled in dancing school at Christmas so I could get all dressed up in a long dress and dance with boys to the music of my era. Uncle always attended these dances and would sit on the sidelines watching the whole event. I was so terrified of getting stuck without someone and have Uncle feel that I was a complete disaster that I would be nervous as a cat at each of these cotillions. But Uncle didn't seem to mind if I danced with the same person for a half hour. One of the dances began with all the boys sitting down in a row and the girls being allowed to run over and ask the boy of her choice for a dance. So all knew then which girl had a crush on which boy!

Uncle loved organizing Christmas dinners. In my early years with the Blairs, he used to have a part of the family come to Blair House for cocktails and lunch. As I grew older, Uncle included more people, eventually inviting the entire Lee family, the Breckinridge Longs, the Montgomery Blairs, Mrs. Woodbury Blair, Mrs. Mitchell with Neddie and Mary, and Bill Blair, Mary Eula and little Billy, their son. It was a gang of us! We held our event at Grasslands, a small club out on Nebraska Avenue, which was the perfect place to have our Christmas celebration. There would be a large tree all trimmed and favors for everyone. It was a lovely family tradition, which I looked forward to each year. When I was about 17, Uncle felt that the time had come for me to run the party. Apparently, I managed to get all the invitations out, order the food, trim the tree, and carry on just as he had done for so many years. I noticed that he was beginning to give me more and more responsibilities. With Auntie getting quite feeble, he needed someone to be his hostess and this was beginning to fall more onto my shoulders. Although Uncle rarely gave large dinner parties, he often had a few friends in and would let me organize the dinner. It wasn't too hard, as I had all the help to rely on and to ask advice from on certain decisions. It was mostly my ideas, however, that were implemented and Uncle seemed pleased.

We always went home for spring holiday in March. My first years at Foxcroft, the spring holiday was uneventful, but the spring break of my senior year was exciting. We spent it in Bar Harbor and up there I was a member of a wonderful group consisting of Lois Thayer, her sisters and brothers, Elinor Pulitzer and her sisters and brothers, Louise Bowen, all the little Moore brothers, Carlyle Cochran and his brother, Prentiss Kent, and countless others. We all did things as a big group without pairing off. We played tennis, swam, hiked, sailed, and went to the local movies on rainy afternoons. We always ended up at Gonga's for the classic milk shake. Flirtations really didn't enter the picture—we were just like brothers and sisters.

Summers were always spent with this group and there was so much going on! Uncle would dress up in his knickers and take off for the golf club. When Auntie could, she supervised the beautiful flower arrangements, ordered all the meals, and then went to the Bar Harbor Club every nice morning around eleven, returning for lunch at one or one-fifteen. Her son, Cousin Franklin, had a house in Seal Harbor. He would come with his family for lunch quite often. Henry, his son, was a little older than I was and I thought him divine. He attended St. Marks, and Yale. I would count the minutes until they arrived. Uncle and Cousin Franklin didn't hit it off too well and would invariably end up in a terrible fight, usually over politics or some moot point, and Auntie would sigh at the other end of the table and say, "Please, Gist, do don't go on so." Cousin Franklin's voice would get more and more agitated until finally he was screaming. Uncle would shout and, wicked girl that I was, I would just sit there loving every minute of such excitement.

Cousin Dorothy came up to run the second house, called "Hillhurst," right next door. Uncle gave her housekeeping money and she bought all the food, hired and fired the help, and of course ordered all the meals. The houses soon filled up with Cousin Monty and Ginney Blair and their children, Aunt Nanna, Cousin Dorothy and her daughter, Margo, and sometimes her sister, Lucille, and Stuart, her son. I guess Uncle got badgered by Auntie to have all of her relatives up for the summer. In our house, there was usually just the Ellises and sometimes Mr. French from the American Security and Trust Company in Washington. Mr. French was the Trust Officer and later managed my trust fund after Uncle passed away. We had few other visitors due to Auntie's worsening condition. I was, however, allowed some house guests when I was in my third year at Foxcroft.

Uncle was deeply involved with the preservation of the park lands on Acadia and he was in charge of overseeing the condition of the paths. He was an ardent walker and climber until it got too much for him. He would often take me for long walks early in the morning. I used to love this. I soon learned to climb every mountain on the island. The family adored going to Jordon Pond for tea. What a beautiful Maine tradition! We would all sit out on the lawn overlooking the "bubbles" at the end of the pond. After a walk around the pond we would find a picnic table and settle down for hot tea and popovers and strawberry jam and ice cream. What a treat! Uncle would know a lot of the other people there and would wander around shaking hands left and right. Auntie would have to sit alone, but a lot of their friends came up to shake her hand and say a few kind words.

Our living room at Cleftstone was still the room where all of the activity was—bridge in the evening, cocktails before dinner, coffee after dinner, and reading by the fire on cold and damp days. I had studied piano, but not nearly enough to really play. I would just amuse myself by playing the four or five tunes I had learned by heart and trying to read sheet music and play with one hand.

Leading off of the living room was a glassed-in porch with lots of black painted wicker furniture. This was the sunny part of the house. Uncle and

Auntie would often sit here in the morning reading the newspapers. John, our gardener, had huge potted plants all over the place. Unfortunately, one summer I took to dumping my breakfast cocoa and milk in the plants, causing them to slowly die. Auntie was very cross with John and made him repot all the plants. Of course, when he did, he found all the decayed food stuff. He never told on me. He just asked me to dump my food elsewhere and he nursed the plants back to health. Thanks to his good gardening, we had flowers everywhere. I loved to watch as John fixed all the flowers every day. Maine in the summer is the perfect climate to grow flowers of all sorts. John would start the flowers out in April in flats, transplant them in May, and by the time we would arrive in July, the flowers were fantastic.

The dining room was an inside room with more of the heavy black wooden furniture. There was a little den on the other side of the dining room where Uncle kept his desk, and the only phone in the main part of the house was in this room. In the den, Uncle had a collection of china creamers in the shape of people, usually ugly but amusing, and they adorned the mantle of the fireplace along with a mantle clock that Uncle was continually winding or resetting. As in Blair House in Washington, this was the room where everyone had to appear at sometime or another to answer questions relating to housekeeping, bills, or social engagements. We all heard a lot of lectures on the subject of "what Laura is doing today." Esther would often have to come to my rescue and try to persuade Uncle that it was quite all right for me to go to the movies with a crowd of kids or go to an early supper party. He was so lost as to what was the correct thing for me to do. His very good friend, Mrs. John Thayer, had five children and she often served as his advisor. Whatever she allowed Lois to do, I also was allowed to do.

The bedrooms on the second level were all furnished in white painted furniture and at the windows were beautiful organdy curtains in white or mauve. Auntie loved all shades of purple and even furnished one of the guest rooms in that color. Her room was pink, Uncle's was blue, and mine, when I came down from the third floor, was all in white. Auntie's room was very large—it was almost a sitting room and bedroom combined. She had a chaise lounge which was piled high with small pillows of all shapes and sizes and covered in lace covers. All of the bed linens were of the finest linen, with a "B" monogram. It was such a luxury to sleep between those soft sheets.

On the third floor, there was a room for Esther and the chambermaid, and at the end of the hall was my room as a little girl, which was all in yellow. There was one bathroom for the three of us. The rest of the staff had their small rooms in the wing off of the second floor. Marcel had the largest, of course, and the head butler had the next largest, then the second butler and the chauffeur. The rooms were small and there was only one bathroom, but no one complained. They seemed perfectly satisfied and could decorate their rooms to suit their tastes. When they got together for a little fun or a party, they gathered in their dining room around a large table. I could come down the back steps to the servants' dining room, which I often did, as in Washington. They tried to teach me to play the guitar and to play cribbage, which was their favorite card game. Listening to Alfred play the steel-stringed guitar was my real amusement, as he was very good. I always spoke French with Marcel and Henri, the chauffeur, and of course when Madame Jeanne and her husband, Rene, were there, and their best friends, Henry and Anna Agneses.

Uncle still chased me out of there as often as he could. It is too bad that he wasn't aware of how much I was really getting out of these visits. However, Henri, the chauffeur, was naughty at times and sometimes when I would have a girlfriend such as Margo Finletter over for a visit, he would try to throw pebbles down our fronts. We thought it amusing, but this tale found its way back to the Damrosches across the woods and as a result, Margo was banned from her visits for a while. We were, after all, growing up and the servants were not to be fresh or too intimate.

When I was 14 and 15, I very much wanted to learn to drive a car. John, the gardener, let me sit next to him and use the gas pedal and steer his old Chevrolet all around on the back roads. When the time came for me to finally get my license at the age of 16, I could drive quite well. Henri taught me to drive the big Lincoln Town Car around, and in the end I used that car to take my driving test in Bangor. We drove over together to the motor vehicle place to take the written test and the road test. The state trooper, amused that such a young girl was taking her test in the family limousine, decided to sit in the back of the car and give me orders through the little car telephone. "Miss Blair, please go around the block one more time, turn right, then left, and then parallel park between those two cars." I was confident and passed without a flaw. The trooper congratulated me and then made me take him for another spin even though I had passed everything. I think he enjoyed being driven around in such an elegant car. After that there was no stopping me! I had to drive everywhere in anything, including cousin Ginney Blair's little black Ford, John's car, Marcel's Pontiac, and anything else I could find. None of my friends were driving yet, so I was in my element.

My most exhilarating moments in Bar Harbor in those last golden summers came as I received swimming prizes. I won all the decathlons at the Bar Harbor Club. I attribute my success in the 60-yard underwater swim to Uncle's cure for hiccups! As a child I seemed to constantly get the hiccups and whenever I did, Uncle would seat me on his lap, take out his watch, and time me as I held my breath. It cured the hiccups and helped me to expand my lungs!

Some evenings I spent at the Club dances; other evenings I spent with Uncle. After dinner at seven-thirty, we would come back to the living room, where there would always be a roaring fire and we would play Russian Bank until bedtime. Auntie would just sit in her chair nodding, until Esther would come and lead Auntie upstairs to settle her for bed. Auntie's Parkinson's disease was progressing and she could hardly get around. I felt so sorry for Uncle, as he was still well and wanted to do more entertaining or go out to dinner, but Auntie just couldn't join him anymore, and out of loyalty to her, he would often turn down a tempting dinner invitation to stay home with her. However, when he did go out, he expected me to be with Auntie and take care of her until his return. I can still hear Auntie calling for Esther or me as she sat alone in her chair unable to rise by herself. When Esther would be out of earshot, I would go to see what Auntie wanted, but sometimes she really didn't know what she wanted. Usually, though, she was calling for help to get to the bathroom. It was sad to see her so helpless, and I would sigh and feel put upon when I had to sit with her or go driving with her all afternoon.

My senior year at Foxcroft I lived at "Sage," which was the senior house. We seniors were situated quite apart from the rest of the school buildings. We had our own living and dining rooms, and three or four girls shared each of the upstairs bedrooms. We felt independent and very superior to the rest of the girls. We did, however, have the responsibility of setting a good example, being leaders, and helping the younger girls adjust to boarding school life. We were certainly adjusted to the routine by our senior year. I was even turning into a good student. I had had a bad time with English literature during my junior year. I was tutored all summer and in the fall of my senior year I was reexamined. I came through with flying colors! I managed to pull all my grades up, in fact, and Uncle was delighted.

Basketball was still my main interest, and I was a forward on the team. My senior year I was in good form and made lots of baskets for the Hound team, and we easily won our Thanksgiving game over the Foxes. Miss Shookie, our coach, was proud of me, as was Miss Charlotte. I also spent a lot of time that fall bike-riding. I had a boy's bike, which I had ridden for the past three summers in Maine. Horseback riding, however, was a dominant activity at Foxcroft. The fall of my senior year, I invited Uncle and Cousin Monty Blair to our Thanksgiving Day hunt and basketball contest.

The hunting girls all went out early in the day and met on the front lawn of Brick House. Uncle had fox-hunted all his life with the Chevy Chase Hunt Club and was delighted to see the beautiful hunters ridden by the master and huntsman and whips all decked out in their hunting colors. Miss Charlotte always rode sidesaddle and was spectacular in her green school habit on a white mare. She rode beautifully and sat as straight as a ramrod in the saddle. We couldn't help but be proud of her even though we all could see that she was aging and becoming forgetful, and sometimes unreasonable. I really excelled that day in order to please Uncle, as he seldom came to any of my school activities. He was too old and the ride was so long.

Mysticism played an interesting role in my senior year. When I was still a little girl, Esther used to play a lot of cards with me. She taught me to "read cards" and tell fortunes. At school I practiced Esther's tricks on my friends. I frequently told fortunes that came true. I often really felt a strange intuition about people and their future, sometimes to the point of not wanting to do a reading at all. I decided I wanted to have my fortune told to me by a professional.

Seniors were allowed a long weekend in the fall. Since we could take friends home with us, I asked my roommate, Henrietta Ryding, to come home with me. She lived in Alabama, so she was glad to have someplace close to go for a few days. Of course, Blair House was not the most exciting place to be, as Uncle and Auntie were both ailing in lots of ways, but we found things to do. We went to every movie we could, and since all the large movie theaters were just around the corner, we could walk to them and then stop for a chocolate milk shake at Liggett's drugstore on the way home.

We also had time to indulge our interest in fortunes. We both had heard of Mrs. McLaren, a noted fortune-teller in Washington. We dared each other to see her and at last called to make an appointment under assumed names. We would never forget this day as long as we lived! I went in first and Mrs. McLaren told me to write down three questions that I wanted her to answer. Of course, I asked what was on every 17-year-old girl's mind: Will I get married? When? Will I have children? She then told me to fold the paper up and stick it in the middle of my palm and then put my hand down on the table. She covered my hand with her own hand. She started out by saying that she was having a hard time with my name. "You seem to have several names. Are you perhaps adopted? I feel that you are living with older people who are responsible for taking care of you and I sense that your first initial is 'L' and that your last is either 'L' or 'B.'" I was flabbergasted and couldn't wait to hear the rest of it.

"Your father will die very suddenly sometime within the year. You will soon meet a young man whom you will eventually marry against your parents' wishes, and you will have four or five children. This marriage will break up when you are in your mid-30s and then you will marry a man 12 years your senior, and be very happy."

She also warned me against going ice-skating with a beau of mine, as he would have a bad fall. My time was up and I thanked her and left. Everything she predicted came true—even the ice-skating bit! I had a date to go to the rink the following night, and sure enough, my escort did have a bad fall and almost broke his back.

Mrs. McLaren told Henrietta that she too was living with elderly parents (which was true), and that she would have a happy marriage and lovely children, but her life would terminate early. Henrietta died of cancer around 1987 at the age of 65.

Our experience kind of "spooked us out," even before it began to come true, but we loved telling everyone about it.

Christmas my senior year I again came home for our usual celebration. There was the large family get-together at Grasslands; the same old artificial tree was once again erected in Auntie's boudoir on the same table as it was done when I first came there as a wee child.

Auntie and Uncle left for Charleston, South Carolina right after Christmas and stayed at the "Villa Marguerita," a famous large white house with columns in front, and, in back, a swimming pool filled with plants. The dining tables were situated around the pool. Esther went along, of course, to take care of Auntie. I was told that I would join them in Charleston for the three-week spring holiday. I was very excited, as I had never been south before, and I had heard a lot about the beauty of Charleston in the spring. Before that lovely vacation, however, I had to live through the most humiliating period of my youth.

With Auntie and Uncle, Esther, and the chauffeur all in Charleston, South Carolina for the winter months, I was alone after Christmas in Blair House until it was time to go back to school. I was lonely and was delighted to be invited to Baltimore for a few days to visit Miss Charlotte's niece, Kitty Smith. I immediately went up by train, never giving a thought to any prior engagement I might have had. I had a glorious time with Kitty and her friends. We especially enjoyed an unexpected snowstorm, which gave us the opportunity to spend endless hours sledding down the hill she lived on.

As I awakened the day after the storm, it suddenly dawned on me that I was supposed to be in Washington for a luncheon at the White House given by the Roosevelts for the "sub-debs." I remembered the invitation said the luncheon was at 1:00, but what I didn't know was that one was supposed to be there promptly at 12:45. I thanked my hostess for a wonderful time and apologized for such a hasty exit, but I knew Uncle would be very upset if I casually bypassed an invitation to the White House. I caught the first train I could but it was delayed by the storm. I arrived at Union Station around 12:45, and thinking I could still make the luncheon, I begged the taxi driver to rush me to the White House. Washington's traffic was a mess and it seemed to take forever to get there. I tipped the driver and asked him to please deliver my suitcase across the street where I lived. He must have thought he had a very eccentric passenger, but he did as he was told. It never dawned on me that I might never see the suitcase again.

I ran into the side door of the White House, and collided head on with one of the aides. He wanted to know where I thought I was going. I said, "I am here for the luncheon, and I realize I am late, but I couldn't help it. The snowstorm made the trains tardy." He tried to talk me out of staying, explaining that no one ever arrived late for a White House function, and I would only embarrass myself and everyone else. I was not to be put off. I begged and pleaded, so he said, "All right, if you must. But at least take off that silly turban, comb your hair, and put some makeup on, and let's hurry upstairs. But remember, you must stand erect and look poised. I shall first take you to the President, then the First Lady, and finally Mrs. Roosevelt, Sr."

I was beginning to regret the whole adventure, but as it was too late to back out, I forged ahead. We walked into the dining room, which was filled with long tables, white table cloths, beautiful china, and all of my friends. I was horrified when I realized that the main course was about to be taken away. I held tight to the aide, and walked as tall as I could. Everyone stopped talking, frozen in complete astonishment, and the only sound were my high heels clicking on the parquet floor. I was presented to the President as promised. He looked up with a mouthful of food, and extended his hand saying, "I am very glad to meet you, but aren't you a little late?"

"I am so sorry, but I was delayed by the snowstorm. I came as quickly as I could."

"I understand completely," the President continued, "but I only hope the others will. Good luck, young lady."

My knees were knocking as I went next to Mrs. Roosevelt. She was very kind and accepted my feeble excuse. The final test was still to come. The President's mother was sitting at another table waiting to pounce on this child who should have known to send regrets if she could not be on time. I gave her the same spiel as the others, hoping she would wave me past.

Instead, she looked me up and down, and said in a very formidable voice, "This is most irregular, and I will see to it that you will never be invited to a White House function again. Now go and take your seat." When I finally made it to my assigned seat next to two of my best friends, I almost burst into tears. The daughter of the Peruvian Ambassador said, "Laura, you are in deep trouble. After lunch you had better come back home with me and we shall ask my mother what you should do to make up for this terrible faux pas." I swallowed three courses at once trying to catch up with the others. After lunch, we all retired to a small room for coffee with Mrs. Roosevelt, and then we were excused.

I did go back with Louise Stillwell, Madame Espil's daughter, to her house, and talked the whole mess through. I was advised to send flowers to the Roosevelts with a letter of apology and two dozen long stem roses to Mrs. Roosevelt, Sr. On top of all of that, I had to send a telegram to Uncle and Auntie in Charleston explaining what I had done so they wouldn't hear of it through the gossip channels. They were horrified, and made no bones about it. Cousin Dorothy was also upset. I was not a very happy "sub-deb." Finally, I did receive a letter from the President and Mrs. Roosevelt thanking me for the flowers and forgiving me, and a separate letter from Mrs. Roosevelt, Sr. stating that my apologies had been accepted, and that I was reinstated on the White House list. Needless to say, I breathed a sigh of relief, and promptly called Uncle up to reassure him all was well. I returned thankfully to school within the week, having learned my first lesson in etiquette. I was never late again anywhere.

Back at school, we had mid-term exams, which I hated, but I managed to pass in every subject. There were some basketball games against other schools for which I still played forward. I also took fencing lessons and tap dancing, which I adored. I even learned a few complicated routines to be executed at graduation.

We always had a big costume party for George Washington's birthday. One year, a pile of us came as his false teeth. I thought it was funny, but Miss Charlotte didn't think so at all, and gave us the booby prize for making fun of him and showing no respect. We had dances and a lot of fun to pass the cold winter months away.

Blair House was nearly closed down during these months, with only the servants living there. I went back in the spring to an empty house to stay for a day before flying to South Carolina. I brooded on having only one more term to go before I would be free and launched into society. I dreaded leaving the school, as it had become such a part of my life, but on the other hand, I wanted parties, and to meet men and to dance the night away. I was learning to apply a little makeup, but Uncle would always notice it and take it right off. He said that he did not want me to look like a "whore." Oh! Our generation gap!

I arrived in Charleston and immediately fell in love with the city. Azaleas, camellias, live oak trees, the water, the cobbled streets, and the single and double houses dating as early as 1720 all charmed me. It was spring and love was in the air. Thus Uncle, taking the advice of one of his newfound friends, asked a certain young man over for dinner with me. Little did he know then that that would seal my fate. We did have dinner, but I wasn't the least bit impressed with the rather good-looking young man. He was shorter than I was, and he smoked cigarettes, dropping the ashes in the cuff of his trousers. How shocking! After dinner, Uncle took us to see the movie, The Last of the Mohicans, at which this blind date of mine promptly fell asleep! I had not had many dates up to this point, so I was a little taken aback. After the movie, we asked Uncle if we could go for a milk shake at the nearby drugstore. Uncle said "no" at first, but then relented, as long as the young man promised to bring me right back afterwards.

Soon after this "date," I was asked out again by the same man and then he began to send me corsages of gardenias. This was a "first" for me. They smelled so good! Although Uncle had met Teddy's parents and seen their beautiful house on Gibbes Street, he became uneasy about my seeing too much of this young man. I did have other dates which were fun, but met lots of Charleston girls. Since Uncle wouldn't often let me out at night, my date asked me if I would join him at dawn and watch the sun come up from the dock of the Yacht Club. That was a new approach and I loved it. We didn't act very romantic, but it was exciting to climb out my window and get picked up at the corner and somehow get back in my room before I was supposed to have breakfast with Uncle. I don't think Uncle ever caught on to my sneaking out almost every morning. Those mornings were wonderful! With the balmy air and all the flowers in bloom, it was like living in paradise.

Uncle expected me to stay home most afternoons and take Auntie for drives. We had our car there and Henri, the chauffeur. I felt sorry for Uncle, as he seemed so lonely and in a way, he seemed a little jealous of my frivolous life. But the time in Charleston passed quickly and before too long, I found myself back at school again. Uncle and Auntie came home to Blair House shortly after I left Charleston. I had one more "weekend" I could take away from school in the spring term. I took it in Washington and spent a lot of time talking to Uncle and Cousin Dorothy making arrangements for my big tea dance in June. Bless Cousin Dorothy, who often visited me at school that spring to continue our planning sessions.

Uncle was very concerned that he was getting too old to continue the running of the house and had high hopes that I would become his hostess and housekeeper after I had fulfilled my obligations as a debutante. He talked to me for hours on how important it was for young ladies to understand how to buy food, manage the staff, pay the bills, and most important of all, keep an accurate list of expenses. I could hardly see myself fulfilling this role so soon out of boarding school, but I knew that he was beginning to depend on me more and more.

The spring term went along smoothly. A highlight was the annual spring horse show. Uncle came to watch me. I entered several classes and won a ribbon or two. In the final days, we all studied hard for our exams and prepared for the graduation to be held in Miss Charlotte's garden. I had bought a plain white dress for the occasion and all was set except the assurance that we had passed! At last the final marks were posted and I passed everything with a B average. The relief was overwhelming, as I had so hoped not to let Uncle down. At the ceremony, Uncle sat with Cousin Franklin Ellis and Ginney and Monty Blair. I did not win any of the scholastic awards, but I did win a social service prize for having been so dedicated. I also was awarded a silver box for the girl who has shown the most improvement in posture during the four years.

My family drove home right after graduation, but we girls all stayed on for the night for a banquet, laughter, and games. It was a tearful day that followed, as we packed all our things and wondered if we would ever see each other again. As I drove off with Henri in our Lincoln limousine, I felt very lonely. I would have been comforted if I could have foreseen a day that even Mrs. McLaren had not seen—when I would see my granddaughter graduated from Foxcroft. While she was there, I visited many times to watch the Fox-Hound basketball games and go to the horse show. And oh! the memories I enjoyed at her graduation.

CHAPTER X.

The Debutante

I was still overcome with sadness my first week back at Blair House. Soon, however, I was in the debutante whirl. I had to begin to buy clothes for luncheons, teas, tea dances, dinner parties, and dances that would last all night. Uncle put me on a clothes allowance of $60 per month. Although the buying power of a dollar was greater then, I still had to watch every penny in order to buy my coming out dress, lots of evening gowns, afternoon dresses, stockings, and hats. Uncle helped with the extra money for a couple of things, but basically, he was intent on continuing my training in learning the value of the dollar.

My debutante year was 1940. Europe was being ravaged by Hitler, and the talk within the family was very depressing. Uncle often told me, "Certainly we will be dragged into a war before too long." But this attitude seemed to hardly touch me or my friends. We felt we were there to enjoy and have fun and dance the night away to the "big band" sound.

Most of the large parties were given at a debutante's parents' home under outdoor tents beautifully decorated in a different theme each night. The music was by Meyer Davis or Lester Lanin and sometimes even Benny Goodman and his band. Not satisfied with all there was planned in Washington, we would often take a train to Baltimore for more of the same. All of my "deb" friends had a mother to help them dress properly, answer all invitations promptly, and shop with them, but not me. Esther did what she could, and Cousin Dorothy showed me how to answer invitations correctly, but the rest was pretty much up to me. I had to keep track of all the luncheons, teas, and dances, and still not get worn out. By the middle of June, the excitement, activity, and work of being "proper" was beginning to make me drag. The biggest dance of the "deb" year was the Tenth Annual "Black and White Ball" held in the Mayflower Hotel ballroom. By the light of a simulated moon, debutantes in white tulle, flowing chiffon, or satin that gleamed in the pale glow were whirled gayly about the floor as Sidney's Orchestra played for dancing. Buds of the season were asked to come in white gowns, set off with a wreath of gardenias in powdered or silvered hair. Post-debs for the most part also appeared in white. All other guests had their choice of black or white. All escorts and extra men wore white tie and tails.

Promptly at 10:30 p.m. two trumpeters in black and white colonial costumes heralded the formal opening of the ball and belles of the season lined up with Mrs. William Laird Dunlop, hostess for the fete, who headed the receiving group. Fifty debutantes of Washington and other cities were in the receiving line and several hundred other guests were in the throng that enjoyed the ball.

Miss Louise Stillwell was first in the line of debutantes and next to her was Miss Peggy Lansdowne. Others in the line included Miss Elizabeth Fish, Miss Elaine Darlington, Miss Sita Finkenstaedt, Miss Alice Ingersoll, Miss Ruth Woodson, Miss Marion Norris, Miss Mary Norris, Miss Elizabeth Stewart-Richardson, Miss Courtney Owen, Miss Catherine Hill, Miss Suzanne Slingluff, Miss Cloe MacDonald, and Miss Sheila Broderick.

Among the hundreds of young men who did their part to make the ball one of the most successful larger fetes of the season were McCullough Darlington, Sydney Kent, Rufus Johnson, Harold Fangboner, Jack Arrington, Robert MacBride, Edgar Prochnik, Capt. Charles F. Harrison, Otis Wingo, Nicholas Gill, Henry Huidekoper, Fred Mechlin, Lt. J.L. Lackes, and many more. Of course, all of these events were written up in the newspapers. On this particular occasion, my pre-party was noted: "As is always the case when a large party goes on the Washington boards a number of dinners preceded the ball. Miss Laura Blair entertained 16 dinner guests at her parents' home on Pennsylvania Avenue."

When the final guest was greeted, the line broke and the debutantes and their beaux swung out onto the floor for the first numbers, "Stay As Sweet As You Are," "Just the Way You Look Tonight," and "Love in Bloom." After those dances, the debutante contingent shared the spotlight with buds, post-debs, and other guests and the ball went merrily along until the early morning hours. At twelve-thirty, supper was served and then dancing to Sidney's Orchestra continued once more.

The main event that Uncle arranged for me was a tea dance, which came off brilliantly. My dress was beautiful. Someone sent me a corsage, and Esther got me the long white gloves, and I stood with Uncle for several hours shaking hands with all of his friends and the young debs and their escorts. I can remember telling Uncle that my hand was about to fall off. I think he was very pleased that night to feel he was doing the right thing for his adopted daughter whom he adored. The music played until six-thirty, when we all had to leave and get ready for another dinner and dance. I gave several small dinner parties at Blair House, which was good practice for starting my new career of running the house. It was well established in Washington society that the men were allowed a drink, but the debs—never! If a deb did drink, she would be eliminated from all the rest of the season immediately. Only as a post-deb could a girl drink in public, as she was considered "on the shelf."

Poor Uncle thought at first that the thing to do each night was to sit up and wait for my return. I would come in extremely late and find him sound asleep in his chair, and I would have to wake him and help him up to bed. He also wanted me up by eight to join him for breakfast. After a few days of this routine, Uncle was half dead and so was I. Ginney Blair and Cousin Dorothy both came down to Blair House and insisted that Uncle go to bed on time with the understanding I would wake him up upon my return. They also got Uncle to agree to let me sleep until at least eleven. Uncle didn't like the plan at all, but due to his age and lack of rest he soon realized that he must listen to their advice. He was so frightened that I would end up at some sleazy night club after the dances were over! It was hard to make him understand that what we really did was all go to the Hot Shoppes and have one of those thick milk shakes that you can't even stir.

We did have one other place where we all congregated called "2400 Conn Avenue." It was sort of a night club but was frequented only by the deb crowd.

During the day, if there wasn't anything planned, we debs and our escorts all met out at the Chevy Chase Club for tennis, swimming, or just sitting around in the sun. The party rush was just about over toward the end of June, when 4:00 p.m. garden parties began. We all wore large hats, and flowing dresses of organdy and tulle. The weather seemed to be always good, though a bit too hot, and the gardens were stunning. Among some of my deb contemporaries were: Peggy Lansdowne, Zevah Fish, Beth Kean, Anne Sperry, Barbara Beale, Elaine Darlington, Anne Huidekoper, Eleanor Neil, Jane Lucas, Nancy Glover, Pat Hurley, the Norris twins, Joan Morgenthau, Jean Wallace, Jean Davis, Sita Finkenstaedt, Betty Stewart-Richardson, Louise Stillwell, and many others.

In July, we all went away from the heat of Washington, and Uncle and Auntie and all the rest of us headed for Bar Harbor, where I continued to have fun. There were no more coming-out parties, but I went to lots of dances at the Bar Harbor Club, and over at Northeast Harbor at the Kimball House. Our routine continued as other summers past. In the afternoon, I would either go driving with Auntie or visit next door where Cousin Dorothy and her children often gathered for the summer, along with the Monty Blairs and their four little girls. I think Uncle enjoyed having the family together, and was fortunate to have bought "Hillhurst" as the guest house right next door to "Cleftstone." Uncle had had his prostate operation and was feeling better, and I had some of my friends up to visit, but Uncle still kept a close rein on me. Before some of the Club dances I was allowed to host formal dinner parties for my friends. Uncle would eat alone with Auntie and I was on my own to enjoy the experience as a hostess. Despite all the growing responsibilities, however, at 18 I was still expected home by 1:00 a.m.

My beau from Charleston asked to come up for a week. He was staying with his family in Falmouth, Massachusetts, working for S.S. Pierce and Company. Uncle was not pleased as he did not want me to become involved with anyone yet, and when I did, he wanted me to fall in love with a son of one of his wealthy friends. But these "desirable" boys were all old acquaintances and we treated each other more like brothers and sisters. Even at 18, we still played tennis together and went out all together. "Necking" was just beginning in our lives. You were either a "free neck" or considered a prude, but no one ever considered going beyond the kissing stage.

We arrived back at Blair House in September, just in time to start going to more parties. It was planned that the Monty Blairs would give me a dinner dance at the Sulgrave Club over the Christmas Holidays. I was thrilled, as that would be the end of my deb year and a wonderful way to wrap up my year. There were even to be some White House parties planned for Thanksgiving and Christmas. I looked forward to a fall of parties, but Uncle had other ideas for me. He announced that I would be attending secretarial school in order to learn typing and shorthand and bookkeeping. He enrolled me at a school to which I could walk, and off I went, even though I wasn't ready to take on more books. I loved the typing and the accounting, but hated the shorthand, as I just didn't seem to be able to take to it. The school gave me my own little Royal typewriter, which I kept on my desk in my bedroom.

The "business" part of life didn't end with school. Every evening after I came home, Uncle put me in charge of the house. I would have to go downstairs and talk to Marcel about menus for the meals. On Saturday morning our chauffeur took me to the market. I was totally confused trying to shop for the large place which I was to run. Although I had been there in years past with Marcel, and remembered how he bartered with the fish man and butcher, I was now all alone and I had no idea what I was buying. I wasn't sure how to tell if the vegetables were fresh, nor did I know how much a chicken should weigh, or what part of a cow became a porterhouse steak. I had even less idea what to do with lamb. I learned hard lessons at first. Uncle gave me $1,000 per week to buy everything, as well as tend to the needs of the rest of the house and pay the servants. He gave me a notebook in which I was to jot down everything and the price I had paid for it. To make me feel under even more pressure, Uncle asked Ginney Blair to come down and check my figures. They were always a little off because, like the servants, I was practicing the fine art of graft. The $60 per month clothing allowance was becoming more difficult to live on. Ginney knew but she never gave me away. She would pencil in correct figures to make the book balance, and I would recopy it before I presented it to Uncle for his inspection.

During those three months that fall, I could date at night, but I had little free time. As well as school all morning and household duties in the afternoon, Uncle spent a long time with me teaching me more about silver and furniture. The butlers taught me how to set the table for different functions, what the china was called, and how to arrange the silver and the linens. Vickie showed me how to clean a bathroom and vacuum the floors and dust the tables and ornaments, and Esther showed me how to iron and sew. Some of these chores came easily to me and some I already knew from watching the staff prepare for parties all my life, but to suddenly find myself in charge was a shock.

No one taught me how to deal with the real problems. How did I tell one of the servants that I didn't think he was doing a good job when all the servants had known me since I was a child? What was I to do when I caught a butler ordering liquor for his own consumption and charging it to Uncle? The problem of widespread and expensive cheating had been going on for years. The servants did not appreciate my snooping around, as they were used to no supervision, and doing as they pleased. Once, the bill from Magruder's (a very fashionable, exclusive grocery store then) showed me that things had been bought or ordered that I knew we had never consumed in the house. I took each servant to task to find out who the culprit was. It was Alfred, the second butler, but since Uncle didn't want the hassle of hiring new servants, I just begged him not to do it again, and to my knowledge, he never did.

Uncle's final days were approaching fast. Although he looked in good health, he had something wrong with his legs which made him limp a bit. A nurse came and went, but he was usually more hale in the evenings. He was up and dressed most of the day and had dinner with me every night. No one told me he had any real illness, just that he was ailing a bit and needed someone to dress him and take care of him. He tried to keep on as usual, especially as Christmas was coming. He wanted me to take over the family party out at Grasslands. The only hint I had of impending crisis was when Uncle called me to his bedside one morning and told me that he wanted to talk seriously to me about my future. First of all, he wanted me to really analyze my relationship with my current beau. He suggested that we not be in touch for a whole year, but if after that, we wanted to get married, Uncle would support our decision. Uncle's second point seemed even odder. He wanted me to promise that whatever money I might inherit from him would not be spent on poor relatives. I had no idea where he got an idea like that! (I found out later it was Percy.) I had hoped to be able to help my mother. I sobbed at the shock of what Uncle said as both restraints seemed so unfair. After sobbing for what seemed hours, I agreed to his proposals of not seeing my beau for a year, and not giving my inheritance away to poor relatives. It was a hard day for me as I left Uncle's bedside, as I felt the burden of maturing and making hard decisions difficult. It seemed at the time that it was the end of the world, but within a week, I found I had other beaux who were pursuing me and I realized I did have a lot of friends and parties to go to which would occupy me during a year of waiting.

That fall the family gave me my first electric Victrola to replace the one that I had to wind up after each record. That fall I seemed to spend all my free hours in the record shops listening to records with my friends. I acquired "Chattanooga Choo-Choo," "Little Brown Jug," "Pennsylvania 6-5000," "Tuxedo Junction," "A String of Pearls," "These Foolish Things Remind Me of You," "Daddy," "Frenesi," "Serenade in Blue," and lots of Johann Strauss, as we all waltzed the night through at least once a week. We also went to hear Benny Goodman, the King of Swing, who just about knocked us cold. We gathered at movie houses which featured the big bands, and sat and listened for hours to "Goody-Goody," "Body and Soul," "Blue Skies," "The Angels Sing," and "One O'clock Jump." Gene Kruppa on the drums was a show-stopper! It was a fast, wonderful, and fun time despite more demands at home, Uncle's health, and the growing problems in Europe.

On December 16, 1940, Colonel Metcalf from the Society of the Cincinnati came to visit Uncle, who was in bed resting. Colonel Metcalf made some proposal to Uncle about the Society of the Cincinnati and Uncle disagreed in his usual way, which was to get hopping mad. Uncle screamed and shouted at Colonel Metcalf so loudly that I could hear him in the front hall as I was about to leave to visit my friend, Peggy Landsdowne. When Colonel Metcalf came down to leave, he said, "My goodness, I have never seen your uncle so mad." I had, so thinking no more about it, I left for Peggy's house. I hadn't been there more than an hour when Cousin Ginney called me to tell me that Uncle had just passed away from an apparent stroke. I was stunned! Even though I had been annoyed with him for his narrow-mindedness and lack of understanding of a child and teenager, I had loved him. I burst into tears, and Peggy's mother took me right back to Blair House. The tone of the house was of great shock and sadness. Poor Auntie had to be told but she didn't understand it all and never quite took it in. When I went to Uncle's room, I was surprised to see that he was sitting up in bed with his hand outstretched as though he was still talking to someone. The nurse had left the room during his conversation with Colonel Metcalf. After Colonel Metcalf left, Uncle summoned the nurse, but by the time she reached him, he was already dead. I had never seen anyone dead before, so I could hardly take it in myself.

For two days Uncle remained in bed, with his arms folded and still in his pajamas. Percy and I lit candles at the foot of his bed, which we kept burning all night long and all day. Finally, the mortician dressed Uncle in a blue suit and laid him in his casket down in the back drawing room. The time had come for everyone to pay their last respects. I was, of course, the "hostess," as Auntie was too ill to attend. I was dressed in black. I met people as they came to the door, shaking hands with everyone and leading them into the parlor to file by the open casket. Uncle looked perfectly natural and very handsome lying there in peace. On December 19th, the funeral services were held at 11:00 a.m. at St. John's Church just across Lafayette Park. We were picked up in the limousines from Blair House, where the family had met so we could all go together. After the service, we drove in a long motorcade to Rock Creek Cemetery, where Uncle was put to rest with his father and brother and other family members in the Blair vault.

CHAPTER XI.

On My Own

The first task I had to arrange after Uncle's death was the formal reading of his will. It was a brilliant instrument that dictated exactly what he wanted done with his property after Auntie passed away. She was to live on another two years, but as ill as she was, it was now my duty to run the house.

The first domestic crisis came when Marcel, our chef, left for another family. After interviewing several candidates, I selected a woman who had been a cook over at the White House. I was impressed at first, but after she settled in I soon realized I had made a mistake. She wanted to cook just about everything in thick cream and use tons of butter. The food was so rich that I could not eat it and it was entirely unsuitable for Auntie. The cook refused to change her style, so summoning all of my courage, I fired her. The next cook was better and put out easy food for just Auntie, the staff, and myself. Henri, the chauffeur, also left, as well as the kitchen maid. We were down to Esther, Vickie, Alfred, a chambermaid, and the cook. My next household task was to hire a new chauffeur. Although I had my own little Ford convertible, we still needed a chauffeur to take Auntie for her drive in our limousine every afternoon.

Christmas was terrible, as no one had their hearts in it. The party for me was canceled and to all the others I had to send my regrets. The minute the New Year came in, several of my friends asked if I felt like going to Florida for a few weeks. I felt the house could run without me for a while and the rest of the family thought so too. The family decided I would be allowed to take up with my beau again so we agreed that the first stop would be Charleston. We spent the night with his parents, who had a grand house. I was glad just to get down to Florida to rest. We took a cottage at Pompano Beach with a chaperone who drove us nuts. We felt that we were mature enough to do as we pleased, but having a chaperone had been a family condition. One day I went up to Palm Beach and visited Marcel, who was working for the Sears family. He asked me to stay and he cooked one of my favorite meals. I loved seeing him. It was a touch of the world that had changed.

Back at Blair House, problems were waiting for me. It was decided by the nurse that Auntie had to have a hospital bed. Esther, as Auntie's chief nurse, had a lot of influence over Auntie and thus, I believe, Vickie started a master plan to do away with Esther. Slowly but surely, Vickie planted suspicions that Esther was writing out checks for herself and getting Aunt Laura to sign them. Auntie could hardly write and she was much too mentally out of it to understand what the checks were for. Some of them were perfectly legitimate. Then Vickie attacked Esther's care of Auntie. Vickie kept telling me that Auntie would lay in her bed for hours with Esther gone and no one around to hear her calling. She needed nursing care at this point, but wasn't getting it from Esther anymore. At least that is what I was led to believe.

Vickie also told me that there was a male visitor staying with Esther on the fourth floor. I knew that the man was the one she had met in Charleston in the spring of 1940. I shouldn't have reported it to Cousin Monty, but somehow thinking I was doing the right thing, I had the Blairs, including Percy, all meet in the library while I "told on Esther." It was felt that Esther had "outgrown" her Blair House days. She had been there since 1920, but now was taking too much advantage of Auntie's condition. In the end they sent for her, and Monty had the unhappy job of telling her that she was no longer needed. She cried and cried and told us how much she loved Auntie and that she had never neglected her, much less misused any of the money. But Monty had made up his mind and considered the case closed. Esther left in a flood of tears, and I was left feeling like a traitor. I honestly did not know whom to believe. I loved Esther, for she had taken care of me as a child, but Vickie had turned me against her. I tried to think of what Uncle would have done under the circumstances. I justified my actions by deciding that since Esther was in love and was going to marry Leon Lackey, her days at Blair House were nearing an end anyway.

Vickie took over the main care of Auntie, and I must say she did do a good job. The summer of 1941, we went as usual to Cleftstone. It was a bit lonely. I was now a young lady who had made her debut, so I went to fewer parties. Uncle was gone and I was left with no one but poor Auntie, who continued to fade each day. I drove around with her each afternoon, and I had my little car so I could come and go at will. There were a few club dances, but basically things had changed in my life and in the world. A lot of the deb parties planned for 1941 were canceled. The buds, debs, and post-debs spent their time working for "Bundles for Britain" or taking Red Cross courses. I took the Red Cross Nurses' Aid course and spent part of each day while I was in Washington making beds and giving baths at the Emergency Hospital.

The following Christmas, the family felt that I should go south and spend it with my beau's family in Charleston. Vickie took Auntie to Aiken, which was close enough for me to drive over and see her. I went over several times to check out Auntie's care and condition. Vickie seemed to be doing a good job, although Auntie was losing touch with reality and hardly knew me. With a heavy heart I drove back to Charleston to be with my future in-laws.

I went back to Washington, where Auntie was moved to the Emergency Hospital. Cousin Percy moved from Blair House to Anderson House, as curator of the headquarters of the Society of the Cincinnati, and I was given a job as Colonel Metcalf's secretary. I was told to move into Ginney and Monty's house on Kalorama Circle. Vickie stayed in command of Blair House with no one there, not even servants.

It was Percy who came up with the brilliant idea of approaching the State Department to buy the house with most of the interior intact, except what was willed directly to me and Auntie's son, Franklin Ellis. As Auntie had passed away in the fall of 1942, there was no reason to keep the house in the family any longer. Cousin Monty had inherited it from Uncle Gist, but he and Ginney had decided that they loved their home on Kalorama Circle and had no interest in moving to 1651 Pennsylvania Avenue. I was to have Cleftstone and all of its contents and a trust fund would be set up for me if the house could be sold. Percy really set it up, and the Government bought the idea of a nice place to put the visiting dignitaries, as their numbers would be increasing as the war continued. The Government agreed to preserve Uncle's magnificent collection of rare books, silver, china, glass, and his antiques. It was just what Uncle would have wanted. For Blair House to have been torn down as Roosevelt had originally planned to do would have been a sin. It was good that Uncle had invited President Roosevelt over one day to see the house and impress him with its historical importance. After that visit Roosevelt promised that, as long as he was in office, he would see to it that nothing would destroy Blair House. Now that it was passing into the hands of the Government, I felt secure that Blair House was in safe hands.

My four months living with the Monty Blairs were the best thing for me, as they gave me an anchor I was sadly missing. Ginney and Monty were always thoughtful and taught me a lot, and I had their four daughters to keep me company. My fiancée sent me a ring in the mail, and we announced our engagement. We were married April 11, 1942. Ginney and Monty went down on the train with me and my matron and maid of honor. My brother gave me away at St. Michael's Church and the reception followed in the beautiful front garden of □6 Gibbes Street.

I went back several times to stay at Blair House with Vickie when there were no foreign dignitaries present. I was often very homesick for the house and wanted to be back living there again. Vickie finally got what she wanted. The Government gave her the title of "Head of Blair House" or the

"Hostess of Blair House," and a fine job she did for many years until her death.

After all this time, it is with great happiness that the house has again found a benefactor in the person of Mrs. Archibald Roosevelt, who has successfully raised enough money to put Blair House in perfect shape again with the help of Mark Hampton, Mario Buatta, Clem Conger, and Cassandra Stone. Uncle and Auntie would be so pleased and happy to see their home looking so beautiful and well cared for.

Top: Original Lincoln car of the Blairs.

Bottom: Laura, Rene Girault (Madame Jeanne's husband), Esther, Madame Staub, and Madame Jeanne.

Top: Laura in Vevey, Switzerland, age 11 (1933).

Bottom: Laura in Vevey in front of Hotel (1933).

Top: Laura in Vevey at swimming club (1933).

Bottom: Laura in Vevey (1933).

Top: Laura in Vevey (1933).

Bottom: Aunt Laura and Gist Blair at Grand Hotel in Cannes, France (1933).

Top: Esther, Laura, and Madame Jeanne in Washington, D.C.

Bottom: Marcel, Esther, Laura, Madame Jeanne, Madame Staub, and Baby Abel in Washington, D.C.

Top: Laura in Washington, D.C., at age 12 (1934).

Bottom: 12th birthday party in Blair House dining room in 1934. (From left to right) Zevah Fish, Jane Lucas, Joan Morgenthau, Anne Rizik, Ann Huidekoper, Laura, Suzie Masten, Nancy Glover, Eleanor Neil, Ann Peters, unknown, and Nancy Beadleston.

Top: New custom-made Lincoln Town Car (circa 1934).

Bottom: Laura, Aunt Laura, and Uncle Gist: Washington, D.C. (1939).

Top: Laura's debut at Grasslands Club: Washington, D.C. (1940).

Bottom: Laura while working at the Society of the Cincinnati, Anderson House, Washington, D.C. (1941).

Top: Laura at a Sunday afternoon "Beer and Scittles Club" touch football game: Washington, D.C. (1941).

Bottom: Laura at front door of Blair House with her dog Rex at age 18 (1940).

Laura at Blair House for the dedication of
U.S. postage stamp of Blair House (1988).

APPENDIX

Excerpts from Uncle Gist's 1920s Travel Diary*

Memorandum made during our travels in 1920.
Laura Blair
Gist Blair
1651 Pennsylvania Avenue
Washington, DC
U.S.A.

June 5, 1920 Edinburgh, Scotland

"We left New York on the S.S. Lapland May 8th, 1920 accompanied by my wife's maid Esther Ekberg who was promised accommodations by the agent in Washington and arriving on board this was not done. Happening to meet Mr. Lindsey, agent of the Red Star Line, and explaining matters to him, he introduced me to the purser, through whom a berth was secured for Esther with 3 others in the cabin. She was in a day or 2 and after another protest permitted to come from the 2nd class, where her cabin was, to eat with the other maids 1st class. Some 50 having tickets were said to have been left on the dock, not being taken on board because there were no accommodations for them. I wrote Hicks, agent at Washington, a full statement of this lack of care, and my own troubles, and C. De Beauford, 1st Secretary of the Netherlands, met me on board and introduced me to Mr. Cramer, Dutch Minister to the U.S. from Holland on board returning to his country, and he expressed the wish we should be at his table. We later found ourselves with him and his wife, and his secretary, an English girl, and Madam De Cartier, wife of the Belgian Ambassador, and altho the weather was bad for a few days it later became good and our passage was much pleasanter for our table arrangements. Mr. and Mrs. Archibald Murray, Mrs. Charles B. Alexander of New York and other friends were on board. Mr. Garry, the American Minister recently appointed to Switzerland, and Wm. P. Euo of Wasn and ourselves soon got together making a party, bridging, talking or taking a cocktail together before dinner. The only unusual excitement of the voyage was heavy seas breaking in two portholes rather close to us one night about 1 o'clock. The glass was slivered into small pieces and the shock was like we had struck a hard substance. I went into the gangway and saw men at work constructing temporary obstructions to prevent further water coming into the portholes through the broken glass. The passengers seemed very quiet and none were out, save those in the state rooms affected. The ship slowed up for a short time. The running was good until we neared the British Channel when we encountered a heavy fog and ran so slow as to indicate danger. A lighthouse was seen on our starboard. We stopped for some two hours and a notice was posted we should not arrive in Southampton until late the next day. The passengers said the ship lost her course in the fog, and that the land seen was off the French Coast. No one knew. Arriving at Southampton May 18th we landed without incident in London, travelling on the Cars with a Mr. Rufus R. Wilson of Boston whom I met onboard. Percy Blair met us at the Station with his mother and helped most invaluably in getting us and my trunks on an American Express truck. All came safely altho Mrs. Day claimed she lost several of hers on the ship, they not having been put onboard in New York. We went to Claridges Hotel, Brook St., London, where Mr. Lanier Winslow of the Embassy had reserved rooms for us. They cost 6 guineas a day—2 single rooms and a bath—and were the most expensive hotel accommodations I have ever had. We hunted London for some cheaper rooms but found none we felt justified in moving into; London was jammed full. During the two weeks of our stay in London we have principally occupied ourselves hunting up old furniture for 1651 Pennsylvania Avenue. We have been to the very best retail dealers of antique English furniture and to date we have bought some purchases of furniture and silver. The American Ambassador invited us to dinner but we were dining with Mr. Domico De Guara, Ambassador of Brazil, that evening and could not go; we went to see them on Thursday afternoon for tea and found plenty of those we know, and a cordial greeting. On one Sunday we lunched at the Middle Temple with Mr. Robert Newton Crane, attending service at the Temple Church at 11 o'clock. He is an old St. Louis friend. We started for Edinburgh on Friday, June 4th, at 9:50 a.m. and arrived here about 7:10 p.m. and have this small apartment at Caladonian Station Hotel.

Today, June 5th, we went to the National Gallery and we saw the grandest collection of Raeburn pictures to be seen. They excelled any I have seen in any Gallery. The following were the best in my opinion—Lord Newton, Mrs. Robert Bell, John Smith Esq. of Craigens, John Wanchope of Niddrie, Mrs. R. Scott, and Monchrieff, whose shimmering red gown or covering was exquisite. Ronald and Robert Ferguson, archers—all by Sir Henry Raeburn, 1756-1823. I was disappointed in the one of Lady Hamilton. The Burns portraits were also a feature. The portrait of his lady love hangs just below his; this is to be seen and appreciated by those who understand the full account not given in the guide book."

June 6, 1920 Edinburgh

"Caladonian Hotel. We have just lunched and found a Scotsman Sunday, a Presbyterian affair. Nothing is open, save the churches. The daylight lasted until about 10:00 p.m. last night. We have seen the sun shining at eight. At five in the morning it is light enough to see. The sun rises tomorrow at 4:33 a.m. & sets at 9:51 p.m. It is so light one can read most of the evening."

June 8, 1920 Edinburgh

"Yesterday passed a quiet day. Sun shone bright. We hired a horse cab at 6 shillings an hour and saw the town, among other places the house where Sir Walter Scott lived, and Old Grayfriars Churchyard, where I found the graves of his father, and also that of Robert Blair father and son; these were in bad state of repair. We came back curiously on a street named Lady Lawson Street, so Laura and I both found evidences of those related to us having lived here. I am just back from a rather careful inspection of the Castle; as we saw Holy Rood Palace yesterday, I saw this alone. It gives evidence of being old but so restored and rebuilt as to permit few but antiquarians to get accurate knowledge of it. St. Margaret's Chapelle is surely almost entirely rebuilt. Yesterday we saw John Knox's house also. It seemed genuinely old altho the guide book states that the town council improvement scheme of 1870 had "wiped out of existence" the old and beautiful substantial houses in the neighborhood."

June 9, 1920 Edinburgh

"Yesterday morning I saw the Castle in the City and enjoyed the view very much. It seems to be mainly a restored castle and the masonry shows the new to be almost the entire work. In the afternoon we drove to Leith, very dirty and uninteresting, and to Portobello and Joppa, which were cleaner but not especially interesting. The sea had a good sea smell which took me back to my own home shores. We then drove to Craigmiller Castle, much the most interesting of the ruins about Edinburgh, owned for several hundred years by the Prestons, and now by another family. An old retainer showed us over the ruin, which remains as it has for years, with no restorations. The masonry and wonderful stone and arch work is worth a trip to see it alone. The country about Edinburgh seems to be owned by about a dozen people. Estates are immense. This Laird is a nephew of the old Laird who died; he does not live here. He and Lord Rasberry, the Duke of Bucclench, the Earl of Hopetown and others own almost all the land about Edinburgh. Oil having been discovered on some of these lands, they take out large sums annually and the deposits of ground and shale are piled high in the air where the drills and mines have been at work. Around the Duke of Bucclench's property runs a high stone wall some twelve or fourteen feet in height over which the passenger of the road cannot see. The small villages near the great estates contain numbers of poor—several were said to be entirely owned by the nearest landed proprietor. I saw very little evidence of discontent but much poverty and somberness. People are not permitted to drive through these landed properties."

June 14, 1920 Edinburgh

"This morning Laura and I went to the Auctioneer, 18 George Street and received the silver bonbon dish, pass boat, 2 pepper castors, marrow scoop, meat skewer, tankard, & two candlesticks (old English Silver) which she bought at the auction & I paid 86 pounds 3 shillings 6 pence for them. I bought a Shetland shawl for mammy's present."

June 25, 1920 Edinburgh

"This morning we drove to Blair Athol, the talk of my early childhood, rather forlorn looking & the Lodge Keeper, "Mr. Stuart," declined to admit us into the grounds. Half a Crown did open his mouth & move his tongue. He said he was sorry but his orders were explicit, that the Duke was really a good fellow and if I would call on him at Eastwood, a small house he was going to move into, just opposite the Hotel on the River Garry, & ask him for permission to come in he thought I would get it. We drove off to see the Falls of Killicraukie & the Wishing Stone & the driveway of a Mr. Moulthy & his Castle, erected on a bet with the great grandfather of the present Duke of Athol & never finished. The Castle has now remained just as it was left but it descended to collateral heirs. It is a huge place. Still standing, however unoccupied, is better than the other one the Duke built, which never arrived at a roof & is torn down now. Apparently both gentlemen bankrupted themselves in trying to win the bet. Returning late in the afternoon I called to see the Duke at "Eastwood," a very small & unpretentious spot for him. The girl who came out to look us over, after the card was sent up, remarked that the Duke was "hanging pictures & would not be quite up to receiving visitors." I told her "being a Blair from America I had come to see Blair Athol & I had not been admitted, and I wished to see his Grace to get into the house & grounds." She retired to tell my story. His Grace soon after appeared in a kilt & most naturally came up & shook me by the hand. I introduced him to Laura & we had a nice chat of a few minutes, during which he assured me we should be admitted to the Castle and grounds tomorrow morning. Weather is fine. This Scotland's country is absolutely the most beautiful of any countryside I have seen. The rhododendrons planted in huge branches about every four hundred feet apart were a feature on one road for a half mile. A certain beech tree forest with its dear loveable leaves on the ground, looking just as if they had been spilled there for the children, will remain long in my memory. These lovely little stone cottages, each with climbing roses of yellow, white or red, or of all three, must make joyful the heart of many a woman weary with toil sitting alongside of her good man in these lovely daylight evenings."

June 28, 1920 Fort William Station Hotel

"On June 26th, 1920, we motored to "Blair Athol" from Hotel Birmam, after starting Esther & the trunks to the station for a train which we were to catch as it passed us at "Blair Athol" en route to Inverness, where we expected to pass the night. We arrived at the Castle gate and Stuart, the Lodge Keeper, opened it with a smile. We arrived at Blair Castle to be met by the Duke, who in person showed us the great house. The front hall was full of weapons of all ages. On the right-hand side as you enter hung the great sword or swashbuckler or claymore that he told us had been used for several hundreds of years in the clan to take off the heads of the guilty B-3. On entering, a bit of feeling of disappointment came over me. It was too small. That did not last long for the endless numbers of rooms were only faced by this front hall & in quite a different way from our custom. We went up some simple stairs and saw by arrangement the rooms seemed to fill all the back space. Ceilings were high and the furniture mainly beautiful Chippendale, a little French & Sheridan. He said after the Revolution of 1745, his ancestry being for Charly, the Castle had been looted & mostly destroyed by the British soldiers so they did not have very much left them & had bought what was there late in the century or in the early 1800s. He showed me a portrait of Mary Queen of Scots given by her to his ancestor which then had a space in the canvas left vacant for her son James the 1st. It had been in due time filled in by a portrait of him. A Raeburn of the famous Scotch piper I also noticed & a beautiful set of 3 pieces of old 15th century limoge—priceless. The Duke said he would sell them to help pay taxes. He mentioned he had 84 Chippendale chairs of a kind that I admired. Full sets of old Sevre. Old needlework covered many of the chairs. He said that he thought that much of it had been done in times past by the members of the family. Some dozens of bedrooms all were furnished with Chippendale high poster beds. I saw one having the largest of claw & ball feet that ever I have seen, & very strong & very beautifully carved. The Duke also showed me two chairs, Chippendale, of the Scale type. They were carved all down the legs like scales of fish or perhaps serpents, & were exquisite. He said for most of this Chippendale he had the original receipts from Chippendale himself. The dining room had been finished in gold & white with a Louis 16th finish, and the mantle had a picture over it as we have mirrors in most of our modern dining rooms. While the china was displayed in several rooms, his china closet was enormous. It may have contained the pieces for use. I noticed Boye & Dresden. The great banqueting hall for the retainers in the olden time was enormous. Flags and ornaments helped its appearance. On each side of the Castle ran small halls 88 feet in length, filled with trophies of the chase, most of them marked with the names of the man who had killed, with the date, etc. There were hundreds of them. Opening into these long narrow halls were rooms used, I suppose, for guests, perhaps servants. The Castle was lighted by electricity and the Duke replied to Laura's question as to how it was heated, by saying it was not heated, "We freeze." The fireplaces were very small. The walls were enormous. The oldest, built in 1200 & something I measured with my cane & found to be over 9 feet thick. That built 200 years later was a little less thick. The Duke said they knew of several secret stairways in the older parts of the walls. We lunched at the little hotel opposite the park, a good lunch & after change of trains arrived at Inverness & stopped at the Caladonian overnight, then motored by Loch Ness to Fort Augustus on yesterday afternoon. The scenery of the lake is fine, but trees affect the view from the road. It is a very narrow road & for 2 motorcars to pass is dangerous. We felt a thrill in passing one as ours came close to the edge of a high cliff & we received a bit of the feeling we should have had if we had tumbled off. We passed the night at the "Lorat Arms." Vile hotel. I saw Lord Astor's shooting lodge sitting high above us on the mountain as I dressed & looked out."

July 3, 1920 Edinburgh

"Laura and I went to the old part of town this A.M. & bought a chest of drawers from George Nielson the root of walnut oyster pattern. Then went to Wilson & Sharp's store where we have bought a Queen Anne tankard & George the 3rd centerpiece & I left the money there for him to pay for the furniture as he will supervise its invoice & being sent to Washington for me.

Mr. Sharp from whom I bought the centerpiece said it was made by a silversmith named Sharpe. The invoice to America was by the American counsel here whose name was Sharpe. The coincidence of my getting this silver was curiously connected with 3 men named Sharpe."

July 6, 1920 London Claridges Hotel, Room 449

"On yesterday we saw antiques & found Wheatby had collected all — even those from Charles who had agreed to ship & deliver to us in New York. Today I went to most of these places trying to straighten the complications & pay the bills. Yesterday afternoon we went to the American Ambassador's where he had invited Americans to tea."

July 9, 1920 London Claridges Hotel

"Yesterday we attended a sale at Christie's auction rooms. We have met so many antique dealers that we felt quite at home... It was not quite acceptable to have anyone but dealers bid altho of course it was an open market. Each dealer had his own little way of dealing which the auctioneer knew."

July 10, 1920 London Claridges Hotel

"This morning we went to Lanygons & saw furniture & then to Mrs. Shamus' new display of Waterford glass on Bond Street where we agreed to buy two large candelabra 200 pounds... This evening we have been to see The Beggar's Opera reproduced at Lyric Hammersmiths exactly as shown in 1728 so far as costumes, etc. Manners and morals have improved since 1728."

July 13, 1920 London

"Most of our time goes in hunting up antiques."

July 18, 1920

"List of our purchases made in London & Edinburgh —
1. Pair of old Sheraton satinwood card tables painted with garlands of flowers by Pergolesi, bought of Frank Partridge, L350.
2. A set of Chamberlain Worcester Dresden China, 40 pcs (marked), bought of Blairman & Sons, L170.

3. One antique silver centerpiece, 4 branches & small dishes, George 3rd, 1762, bought of Daniel Smith & Robert Sharp, Edinburgh; London makers, L170.
4. An antique silver tankard, Queen Anne, 1713, Edward Pearce, London makers L78.18, bought of Wilson & Sharp, Edinburgh.
5. One Sheraton mahogany inlaid show cabinet owned by Lord Howe & bought & sold to us by J. Rochelle Thomas L125, a period piece.
6. An old lignum vitae coffee mill, L4.
7. An antique old mahogany knife box, sloping front silver mounts, several worked with original London hallmarks but all not so old, L22.10, bought of Owen Even-Thomas, London.
8. One old mahogany boot rack and one old mahogany Hogarth chair, L53 3 sh., bought of F. W. Splaight Hatfield, Hartfordshire, both period pieces.
9. Pair of old Waterford table lights, 1780, Adams design, L200, guaranteed & bought through Fine Arts Society, 148 New Bond Street, of collection of Mrs. E. Graydon Starners.
10. One round table bought through Sir Algernon Craig at the Shops of Lord Roberts Memorial Workshops for disabled soldiers & sailors, 122 Brompton Road, said to have belonged to Lady Walsely — bought on faith & our judgement for L31.
11. Bought of C. J. Charles London & N.Y., an old Queen Anne Walnut bureau (domed), L265, and an old Chippendale mahogany tripod pole screen, old needlework panel & 2 old carved mahogany Chippendale single chairs, claw & ball feet, 1 finely carved old Chippendale armchair, ditto L375 — also small old mahogany chip coffee table with fret gallery, L35, & 2 old turned frame walnut stools covered with old needlework, Cromwellian period, L75 — total L795 — ☐all guaranteed — also 2 Jacobean chairs & one old settee for our ☐tapestry, L150.
12. One old root of oyster pattern commode of Wm & Mary period, bought of George Nielson, Edinburgh, piece guaranteed, $49.10.
13. One inlaid Sheraton mahogany & satinwood Pembroke table (wheel pattern) & one inlaid satinwood armchair made by Henry Blundale, 1788, & signed, bought of Monday Kern & Herbert, L150.
14. One pair antique Wm & Mary torchères, L36. One fine antique Chip. mirror formerly at Burton Pynsent & made by Chippendale himself for Pitt, Earl of Chatham, L110, & 2 antique Hip stuffed back armchairs, L45, bought of Mallet & Son, 40 New Bond Street, London, & guaranteed of the period — also as the facts above

stated, 2 mahogany single Chip. chairs bought from Lenygon & Morant, 31 Burlington Street, London.

15. 2 silver candlesticks of about 1760 — like Hancocks. 1 Geo 3rd tankard changed & somewhat altered, 1 maroscoop, 1 skewer, a wooden pair of pepper cruets, & a candy dish, and one pap dish, old Edinburgh make, all bought at auction, Dowell auctioneer. The English silver has the hallmarks, cost L86+."

July 24, 1920 Paris Hotel de France, etc.

"I commenced reading the Bible May 19th & have read it carefully since during leisure & odd times & am now today in the book Nehemiah p. 543 being deeply impressed & interested & having my faith as well much improved. We really do very little. Laura seeks clothes & hats. I have not done even that. Met Damrosch the musician yesterday who gave me an entertaining account of his tour of Europe with 100 musicians. Many are Russians & a few Germans & Austrians & Italians etc. Their passports must be used everywhere. He employed a man to do nothing else. All have lived in America many years & had their first papers. He said their keen love for the country & pride in it was pathetic. We visited Napoleon's tomb this afternoon & in some building saw a collection of Common arms from the time of the last war — also the flags & aeroplanes etc. & a memorial to the Americans who lost their lives flying & quantity of other odds & ends promiscuously collected in two or three rooms."

July 26, 1920 Paris Hotel de France, etc.

"On yesterday morning we started from here in a motor to see parts of devastated France taking Esther [Laura's maid] with us. We motored along the Paris road to Meaux soon after crossing the Marne River and taking the road to the left soon after crossing the bridge drove direct to Belleau woods, where we inspected the cemetery containing so many of the American boys lost in the fight. Many of the Marines are buried there also of the 26th. It was well kept up & an American flag flying to be seen at a distance. The few boys had different kinds of crosses. The only stone I noticed was to Donald C. Dunbar L. 101st Inf. U.S., Killed July 20, 1918. All others had the simple wooden cross. From this place after viewing the woods above us we went to see the church of Lacyle-Bocage in the little village & found it almost exactly as the picture represented it after the struggle excepting the debris was cleared. And the picture is a good one. Lee Captain Paul C. Harpers little Guide was recently published. I picked up several small bullets in the near neighborhood. Talked with several of the women who said many American soldiers but few tourists had been there. We saw none ourselves. We then went to Chateau Shierry where we lunched at the restaurant Du Cyne, the same I lunched at some years ago the year Woodbury married [1909]. Oh what a change. The wreckage of buildings is great. Climbed to the top of a hill on which is an old Chateau — wonderful view. Saw the bridge across the Marne where such fierce fighting occurred. Easily had a vision of how the armies stood & the fighting occurred by studying the slant of bullets and shells in houses & trees & thinking it over. The little town of Bouresches lying on the road before one reaches Chateau S. is a terribly smashed up little town. Continuing on our trip towards Reims we saw Fere lu Sardenois, Fismes, & some other towns all most dreadfully destroyed with poor people apparently without hope just dwelling in temporary shacks & cultivating the surrounding fields. We arrived late at Reims & after some trouble found rooms at the restaurant called La Madelon, 159 Rue de Vesle, where the landlady said she cooked, the nephew waited, & a niece helped. One hired girl tended the party. We were kept awake most of the night by a barking dog that was said to be watching a butcher's shop opposite. Of some 13,000 houses only a few remain uninjured. The streets are simply a scene of desolation. We saw the Cathedral this A.M. I purchased a number of the pieces of stained glass windows — some of the 14th Century, some of the 17th Century. It has a wonderfully beautiful ethereal look in its desecrated dress just as the Bosche has left it. After restoration it will not be so beautiful. All of the windows are gone and the pictures of it are exact. I contributed to the purchase money for the glass for restoration. The theater on the Emineile Visares opposite is very grand in its ruins also. The poor old hotel exactly opposite the Cathedral where I last stopped the year before the war is wrecked. From Reims we took a course to Soissons & en route inspected A. E. F. Cemetery No. 608. M.H. Hanna, caretaker. In good order. I noticed many wooden crosses had in their center the identification tag nailed to them with a little staple. The owner was buried beneath the cross. Noted Samuel Hicks & Ted M. Rea Co. M.K. Inf. Shortly after on the road we picked up a French helmet. The driver said the grave was there as he passed shortly before. They had dropped the helmet. We carefully went through Berry-au-Bac where the enormous double mines had been exploded burying some 1800 men in the crater. French had mined their underground posts & had in turn undermined the French mining party & all had gone off at one & all had been buried together. The Chemin des Dames hills are visible and the great battlefields far & wide also from these mines & craters' tops. I bought a German helmet from a woman on the ground.

Trees & houses are nonexistent from here on except for ruins. An Italian cemetery was passed also — the Chateau said to have been owned by the man whom Mdme Calloit killed & occupied by Prince of Bavaria. We looked through its wrecked grounds. Its noble great iron fence is smashed & the piles of munitions on the roadside, many still good & unexploded, were left by the Germans. A great sight was had of the fields adjoined No Man's Land on which the tangled wires of both armies, the trenches, foxholes & many little graves, were apparently just as they had been left except for the rust & the green grass. As far as the eye could view one saw this kind of thing. No cultivated field, no cottage nor peasant, nor as we saw it, invading tourist save ourselves looked upon this scene of destruction. I went down into some of the earth holes near Berry au Bac & saw where men slept so as to fight the battles of their country. No sinecure on sleep. We motored through towns among which I remember Port a Vert, Vailley, Conde S Aisne & others on the Aisne River, all sad, poor, destroyed things that made one's heart bleed. German signs were often seen & I noted these Bosche changed the names of the streets of the dear little towns they held — to further insult & crow it over their conquered people, I presume. Muzenbach Strasse. Werner Strasse I wrote down in Vailley. At Soussins we lunched at Hotel de Leon Rouge II Rue de la Gare, a new place. The little black-haired clerk said it was all new except the outside. The buildings here are terribly smashed up & the cathedral is a miracle in that it stands. Two great upright pieces of the tower run alone high in the air. The rest is gone. Why they stay is indeed wonderful. It looks as if any wind or storm would blow them over & kill a few more people. In the church I noted the old books were where one could steal them & a pile of the old leaded glass in the corner. Among the books I saw an old copy of the works of Saint Augustine & one of Missals. In all these damaged Cathedrals collections were being made to restore them. After leaving Soissons we arrived at this Hotel two minutes before eight & I lost $1 to Laura on the time we should get back. Oh how tired I am."

August 13, 1920 Etretat

"Have taken my French lesson, read & studied most of this day. Read the Bible to p. 696. Played bridge last evening with a Mr. Voule, an Englishman who said he was in charge of English soldiers in Holland during the War who as prisoners or otherwise were there & interned. The misery of Germans to prisoners during the early days of the War were indescribable. He said that he had quite recently been to Berlin on business for the English

Red Cross, and that everywhere he was treated with manifest courtesy. In a train full of German soldiers this had been his experience. He is too plainly English for even a German to mistake his nationality. Filed three photographs of us all with the mayor to secure our cards d'indentite this A.M."

August 25, 1920 Etretat

"My sciatica has greatly improved; so has the weather. Time passes very rapidly with nothing new or interesting. French lessons each day, a walk, arrival of the newspapers at two o'clock after luncheon. French, English & American paper all small but with a pleasant few minutes reading. About 4 p.m. we roll to the Casino because I play no more golf on account of my pains & baccarat from five-thirty until a little after seven, then back to the Hotel, dress for dinner & after dinner we play bridge.

Sir Chas. and Lady Jessels & Mr. and Mrs. Voule English, a Miss Yorkes, American & the Murrays form the party."

September 1, 1920 Douai Night

"We have just arrived here in a drizzling rain after a run from Amiens which we left this morning about eleven. We passed through Villers — Bretonneux, Progart, Chuignes, Villirs-Carbonnel, Péronee, St. Queutine, Bellicourt & Cambriar. A few K. from Proyart we stopped and saw the Big Bertha used to shell Amiens. Still just as it had been captured by the Australians in 1918. We met an English officer there who graciously explained the gun, showing me the iron in the crude shape of which part is made which passed the virtue to stand the terrific pressure against the sides of the gun when it discharged. He said had it not been for the discovery by the aeroplanes of the gun & its being knocked out it would have ruined Amiens. The gun is fired by machinery after all around leave it. The trees under which it was camouflaged remain the same. We lunched at Péronne in a little workman's drinking restaurant, having a basket lunch brought with us & buying coffee only. The women talked a lot of their suffering while the Bosche held the town, having to work as slaves for a sou a day and all that was raised being taken by them while they received the slimmest rations. The Bosche were polite to them while they did what they were told. All these towns are terribly bombed, and said to have been uselessly so. We saw the Cathedral at St. Quintain in which was posted a sign stating it had been mined for destruction which was prevented only by the unexpected arrival of the French forces 24 hours sooner than they had been expected.

The Cathedral is being repaired but it is greatly damaged. On the roads were great quantities of war materials. "Ordinance dumps" containing every imaginable object but all well the worse for the weather and time. A large pile of Bosche helmets & English & American helmets failed to tempt me to take any away as a souvenir since they were rusty & the camouflage washed away by rains. The American Cemetery at Boni is 3K off the main road. Some 1700 lay buried in it. The place seemed well kept. A.M. Moonly in charge told me Gen. O'Ryan from N.Y., who had commanded the N.Y. Division from which so many of the dead had come, had been there to see how their graves were being cared for. He complained about the gas still affecting the soil so as to prevent it becoming good sod. Cambrai is less destroyed than some of the other towns altho what did occur there was absolutely wanton & done as the Bosche left. We saw a number of factories which had been destroyed & the machinery taken away by the Bosche was said to have been done without necessity. This town is not attractive & the Hotel vile. The porter said the Bosche had taken all of the carpets when they left. These have not been replaced. There is no sitting room and the "Bureau" is in the Café. I feel quite sure the Bosche, whose sins I have no wish to minimize, did not take away the sitting room."

September 2, 1920 Grand Hotel Bellevue

"We motored from Donai here today. The sun shone & the day was fine. We came through Lens, Loos, Vermelles, Hulluch, La Bassee, Estaires, Armentierres, Bailleul, Loere, Kennel, Messines, to Ypres, from there here. It almost seems impossible to describe what we saw. Many villages cluster along the route which is one of endless desolation. We crossed the frontier into Belgium at Bailleul — near it was a magnificent Chateau in ruins said to belong to the Baron de Pagr on the Belgian side. At a poor little place on a crossroad we were shown the original of the Christ in the trenches. A beautiful & natural face; oh so sorrowful. The broken cross lay beside him while the figure was attached to the old & broken shaft only. An old peasant woman came up to us while we were gazing at the figure & said sweetly & simply "that is the Christ in the trenches." A bullet had pierced the breast. The face might be of an American or any present day nation. I see its great artistic merit. The village was here — Chappelle — & is all in ruins, so a proper setting for the Christ. We lunched at Pont de Neppe, not far from Armentierres in a little shop for drinks. The two little French girls who set our table said their grandfather & mother owned all the land in the vicinity and had a villa farm. He had been accused of being a spy by the Bosche, & taken to Germany while ill & died there. Their home

& all they owned & it contained had gone. The little place in which we lunched was made of the refuse & iron from the guts left by the army. A dog named "Snowey," a white fox terrier, was their pet. An English soldier had given him to the little girl when he left for England after being demobilized & she said he had cried & moped for his master when he had gone away. "Snowey" knew English & immediately attached himself to an English chauffeur. At Ypres we inspected the Hall & town on foot & also sent a postcard to all the family. It is being reconstructed rapidly. The Belgians show greater reconstruction power & have more men to work with than the French. The Avenue des Cemetieres des Tanks is still a very real one. On each side still lay innumerable great tanks, rotting & rusting & just as they were put out of business by the Bosche guns. It is a terrible sight & the landscape for miles portrays the terrific struggles. Trees & fields are still ragged & by their looks compare with what one would expect, only ever so much more. The fields for miles are still without crops — only men are at work in numbers of places filling in the shell holes, cleaning out the wire, and getting ready for another season. Innumerable towns are only to be recognized by their signposts & the crossroads & the foundations of houses. The settlers in all of the places occupied at all live in tiny shacks, but some of these are attractive, having flowers in their yards. The frequent uses of the iron tops of the huts of the soldiers for these newly constructed homes will make a lasting mark in the architecture of the future. These are round & often have walls where I have placed a & b; they are raised up & higher than when used as soldiers' huts & this gives the cottage better air, light, etc. The iron goes into everything, the fences, barns, floors, & new construction will show it for many years to come — the Bosche iron is much heavier & is called by the English, "Elephant iron." This is a nice new Hotel. The coal mines are being rapidly repaired altho their destruction was so scientifically done by the Bosche that the larger mines will require a year & perhaps two before they can be fully operated. They have nice little cottages & Supt.'s offices & houses & work is shown everywhere. Armentierre & Lius are ruined. It does not seem possible that many of these towns can even come back. Where coal can be mined or good land give value to farms people will come & live, but where factories existed & all is gone why should their sites be again renewed unless some special reason exists for it? Also in these cases after all the people who depended on these factories are gone."

September 11, 1920 Paris

"Laura & I had a birthday yesterday. Mine was my 60th so I am ambling now along the road of life with the majority of the milestones far behind me. We dined with Mr. & Mrs. Schoellkof at 10 Rue de Raymond where the marriage contract of Napoleon 3rd and Queen Eugene was displayed. On the day before yesterday Laura & I went to the Luxembourg. I was very disappointed. What has happened — have I or it changed? The pictures all seemed so much poorer that I used to think them. I found my two dear ones, "Souvenirs" & "la Jeunne Fille" by Chaplin. What a joy it is to have sweet memories. There they hung as if of yore. I could not but feel much the same pleasure over them as I formerly had, & yet I do not care for modern art any more as I used to care for it. The old is so much more deep in reaching down to you."

September 12, 1920 Paris

"A beautiful summer day. We drove a short time in the Bois late this afternoon. It was overflowing with the people, all manner & kind of folk with children & their baskets. The Champs Elysees was so crowded with cabs & vehicles that in places one could scarcely drive other than in the line — but what a change, few handsome turnouts of any kind & no horses nor fashionably dressed women. The world is now of the lower middle class in these Paris streets & the fashionable seem to hide themselves in the Ritz Hotel or elsewhere."

October 7, 1920 On board R.M.S. "Adriatic" White Star Line

"We left Paris yesterday by train leaving at 9:45 A.M. — everything nicely managed. We had the managing director & what appeared like all the servants at the France et Choiseul to "see us off" & say "bon voyage." I had paid most of them "pourhois." I was inclined to think they wished us well. Nannie & Walter Wilcox also came to tell of their trip to Verdun. As Laura thought she had found just the one and only bracelet watch at Cartiers that she should ever want in this life we four started just before six o'clock & took a cab & rushed there "to see it". These little incidents with the incoming of packages & the "requests" for payment of bills that accompanied these deliveries contributed to much pleasant general turmoil and excitement & such as even departing voyagers do not always have. However, it was not at all unpleasant and the many little joys of the farewells of friends and of essentially French people such as we had at the France et Choiseul really tint one's emotions with some harmonizing colors that are apt to leave a lasting picture in one's memory for future reference & pleasure. An uneventful journey on the train landed us at Cherbourg where we waited the unpacking of our trunks for a French inspection. They looked in the baggage for gold & for antiques. These latter like the former cannot go out of France legally. Their age is when they date before 1830. It would have been vastly amusing had we not felt the petty annoyances which the inspection included. A very fine inspector in fine uniform began searching my hand satchel. A rich American would naturally I suppose be carrying gold and antiques out of France along with his toothbrush & pajamas. I took out ten francs so he could see me do it. The searching stopped immediately, & our innumerable hand satchels & 8 trunks were promptly marked for transfer to the tender unopened and he secured the ten francs which was less than I paid the transfer porters. Yesterday morning before taking the train I stopped at Cartiers & bought Laura the watch which she seemed to believe possessed the charm to give her every future happiness. I wish some little object had that charm for me. How different we are made. It gave me great pleasure to give it to her & to see her happiness —"

* Background and historical information in Chapter I is from United States Department of State, Blair House, Past and Present: An Account of its Life and Times in the City of Washington (1945).

* Gist Blair's original handwritten diary was found behind some books in the Blair House library in 1988 during the renovation of Blair House.

"INSERT A

Memorandum made during our travels in 1920.
Laura Blair
Gist Blair
1651 Pennsylvania Avenue
Washington, DC
U.S.A.

June 5, 1920 Edinburgh, Scotland

"We left New York on the S.S. Lapland May 8th, 1920 accompanied by my wife's maid Esther Ekberg who was promised accommodations by the agent in Washington and arriving on board this was not done. Happening to meet Mr. Lindsey, agent of the Red Star Line, and explaining matters to him, he introduced me to the purser, through whom a berth was secured for Esther with 3 others in the cabin. She was in a day or 2 and after another protest permitted to come from the 2nd class, where her cabin was, to eat with the other maids 1st class. Some 50 having tickets were said to have been left on the dock, not being taken on board because there were no accommodations for them. I wrote Hicks, agent at Washington, a full statement of this lack of care, and my own troubles, and C. De Beauford, 1st Secretary of the Netherlands, met me on board and introduced me to Mr. Cramer, Dutch Minister to the U.S. from Holland on board returning to his country, and he expressed the wish we should be at his table. We later found ourselves with him and his wife, and his secretary, an English girl, and Madam De Cartier, wife of the Belgian Ambassador, and altho the weather was bad for a few days it later became good and our passage was much pleasanter for our table arrangements. Mr. and Mrs. Archibald Murray, Mrs. Charles B. Alexander of New York and other friends were on board. Mr. Garry, the American Minister recently appointed to Switzerland, and Wm. P. Euo of Wasn and ourselves soon got together making a party, bridging, talking or taking a cocktail together before dinner. The only unusual excitement of the voyage was heavy seas breaking in two portholes rather close to us one night about 1 o'clock. The glass was slivered into small pieces and the shock was like we had struck a hard substance. I went into the gangway and saw men at work constructing temporary obstructions to prevent further water coming into the portholes through the broken glass. The passengers seemed very quiet and none were out, save those in the state rooms affected. The ship slowed up for a short time. The running was good until we neared the British Channel when we encountered a heavy fog and ran so slow as to indicate danger. A lighthouse was seen on our starboard. We stopped for some two hours and a notice was posted we should not arrive in Southampton until late the next day. The passengers said the ship lost her course in the fog, and that the land seen was off the French Coast. No one knew. Arriving at Southampton May 18th we landed without incident in London, travelling on the Cars with a Mr. Rufus R. Wilson of Boston whom I met onboard. Percy Blair met us at the Station with his mother and helped most invaluably in getting us and my trunks on an American Express truck. All came safely altho Mrs. Day claimed she lost several of hers on the ship, they not having been put onboard in New York. We went to Claridges Hotel, Brook St., London, where Mr. Lanier Winslow of the Embassy had reserved rooms for us. They cost 6 guineas a day—2 single rooms and a bath—and were the most expensive hotel accommodations I have ever had. We hunted London for some cheaper rooms but found none we felt justified in moving into; London was jammed full. During the two weeks of our stay in London we have principally occupied ourselves hunting up old furniture for 1651 Pennsylvania Avenue. We have been to the very best retail dealers of antique English furniture and to date we have bought some purchases of furniture and silver. The

American Ambassador invited us to dinner but we were dining with Mr. Domico De Guara, Ambassador of Brazil, that evening and could not go; we went to seem them on Thursday afternoon for tea and found plenty of those we know, and a cordial greeting. On one Sunday we lunched at the Middle Temple with Mr. Robert Newton Crane, attending service at the Temple Church at 11 o'clock. He is an old St. Louis friend. We started for Edinburgh on Friday, June 4th, at 9:50 a.m. and arrived here about 7:10 p.m. and have this small apartment at Caladonian Station Hotel.

"Today, June 5th, we went to the National Gallery and we saw the grandest collection of Raeburn pictures to be seen. They excelled any I have seen in any Gallery. The following were the best in my opinion—Lord Newton, Mrs. Robert Bell, John Smith Esq. of Craigens, John Wanchope of Niddrie, Mrs. R. Scott, and Monchrieff, whose shimmering red gown or covering was exquisite. Ronald and Robert Ferguson, archers—all by Sir Henry Raeburn, 1756-1823. I was disappointed in the one of Lady Hamilton. The Burns portraits were also a feature. The portrait of his lady love hangs just below his; this is to be seen and appreciated by those who understand the full account not given in the guide book."

June 6, 1920 Edinburgh

"Caladonian Hotel. We have just lunched and found a Scotsman Sunday, a Presbyterian affair. Nothing is open, save the churches. The daylight lasted until about 10:00 p.m. last night. We have seen the sun shining at eight. At five in the morning it is light enough to see. The sun rises tomorrow at 4:33 a.m. & sets at 9:51 p.m. It is so light one can read most of the evening."

June 8, 1920 Edinburgh

"Yesterday passed a quiet day. Sun shone bright. We hired a horse cab at 6 shillings an hour and saw the town, among other places the house where Sir Walter Scott lived, and Old Grayfriars Churchyard, where I found the graves of his father, and also that of Robert Blair father and son; these were in bad state of repair. We came back curiously on a street named Lady Lawson Street, so Laura and I both found evidences of those related to us having lived here. I am just back from a rather careful inspection of the Castle; as we saw Holy Rood Palace yesterday, I saw this alone. It gives evidence of being old but so restored and rebuilt as to permit few but antiquarians to get accurate knowledge of it. St. Margaret's Chapelle is surely almost entirely rebuilt. Yesterday we saw John Knox's house also. It seemed genuinely old altho the guide book states that the town council improvement scheme of 1870 had "wiped out of existence" the old and beautiful substantial houses in the neighborhood."

June 9, 1920 Edinburgh

"Yesterday morning I saw the Castle in the City and enjoyed the view very much. It seems to be mainly a restored castle and the masonry shows the new to be almost the entire work. In the afternoon we drove to Leith, very dirty and uninteresting, and to Portobello and Joppa, which were cleaner but not especially interesting. The sea had a good sea smell which took me back to my own home shores. We then drove to Craigmiller Castle, much the most interesting of the ruins about Edinburgh, owned for several hundred years by the Prestons, and now by another family. An old retainer showed us over the ruin, which remains as it has for years, with no restorations. The masonry and wonderful stone and arch work is worth a trip to see it alone. The country about Edinburgh seems to be owned by about a dozen people. Estates are immense. This Laird is a nephew of the old Laird who died; he does not live here. He and Lord Rasberry, the Duke of Bucclench, the Earl of Hopetown and others own almost all the land about Edinburgh. Oil having been discovered on some of these lands, they take out large sums annually and the deposits of ground and shale are piled high in the air where the drills and mines have been at work. Around the Duke of Bucclench's property runs a high stone wall some twelve or fourteen feet in height over which the passenger of the road cannot see. The small villages near the great estates contain numbers of poor—several were said to be entirely owned by the nearest landed proprietor. I saw very little evidence of discontent but much poverty and somberness. People are not permitted to drive through these landed properties."

INSERT B

June 25, 1920 Edinburgh

"This morning we drove to Blair Athol, the talk of my early childhood, rather forlorn looking & the Lodge Keeper, "Mr. Stuart," declined to admit us into the grounds. Half a Crown did open his mouth & move his tongue. He said he was sorry but his orders were explicit, that the Duke was really a good fellow and if I would call on him at Eastwood, a small house he was going to move into, just opposite the Hotel on the River Garry, & ask him for permission to come in he thought I would get it. We drove off to see the Falls of Killicraukie & the Wishing Stone & the driveway of a Mr. Moulthy & his Castle, erected on a bet with the great grandfather of the present Duke of Athol & never finished. The Castle has now remained just as it was left but it descended to collateral heirs. It is a huge place. Still standing, however unoccupied, is better than the other one the Duke built, which never arrived at a roof & is torn down now. Apparently both gentlemen bankrupted themselves in trying to win the bet. Returning late in the afternoon I called to see the Duke at "Eastwood," a very small & unpretentious spot for him. The girl who came out to look us over, after the card was sent up, remarked that the Duke was "hanging pictures & would not be quite up to receiving visitors." I told her "being a Blair from America I had come to see Blair Athol & I had not been admitted, and I wished to see his Grace to get into the house & grounds." She retired to tell my story. His Grace soon after appeared in a kilt & most naturally came up & shook me by the hand. I introduced him to Laura & we had a nice chat of a few minutes, during which he assured me we should be admitted to the Castle and grounds tomorrow morning. Weather is fine. This Scotland's country is absolutely the most beautiful of any countryside I have seen. The rhododendrons planted in huge branches about every four hundred feet apart were a feature on one road for a half mile. A certain beech tree forest with its dear loveable leaves on the ground, looking just as if they had been spilled there for the children, will remain long in my memory. These lovely little stone cottages, each with climbing roses of yellow, white or red, or of all three, must make joyful the heart of many a woman weary with toil sitting alongside of her good man in these lovely daylight evenings."

June 28, 1920 Fort William Station Hotel

"On June 26th, 1920, we motored to "Blair Athol" from Hotel Birmam, after starting Esther & the trunks to the station for a train which we were to catch as it passed us at "Blair Athol" en route to Inverness, where we expected to pass the night. We arrived at the Castle gate and Stuart, the Lodge Keeper, opened it with a smile. We arrived at Blair Castle to be met by the Duke, who in person showed us the great house. The front hall was full of weapons of all ages. On the right-hand side as you enter hung the great sword or swashbuckler or claymore that he told us had been used for several hundreds of years in the clan to take off the heads of the guilty B-3. On entering, a bit of feeling of disappointment came over me. It was too small. That did not last long for the endless numbers of rooms were only faced by this front hall & in quite a different way from our custom. We went up some simple stairs and saw by arrangement the rooms seemed to fill all the back space. Ceilings were high and the furniture mainly beautiful Chippendale, a little French & Sheridan. He said after the Revolution of 1745, his ancestry being for Charly, the Castle had been looted & mostly destroyed by the British soldiers so they did not have very much left them & had bought what was there late in the century or in the early 1800s. He showed me a portrait of Mary Queen of Scots given by her to his ancestor which then had a space in the canvas left vacant for her son James the 1st. It had been in due time filled in by a portrait of him. A Raeburn of the famous Scotch piper I also noticed & a beautiful set of 3 pieces of old 15th century limoge—priceless. The Duke said he would sell them to help pay taxes. He mentioned he had 84 Chippendale chairs of a kind that I admired. Full sets of old Sevre. Old needlework covered many of the chairs. He said that he thought that much of it had been done in times past by the members of the family. Some dozens of bedrooms all were furnished with Chippendale high poster beds. I saw one having the largest of claw & ball feet that ever I have seen, & very strong & very beautifully carved. The Duke also showed me two chairs, Chippendale, of the Scale type. They were carved all down the legs like scales of fish or perhaps serpents, & were exquisite. He said for most of this Chippendale he had the original receipts from Chippendale himself. The dining room had been finished in gold & white with a Louis 16th finish, and the mantle had a picture over it as we have mirrors in most of our modern dining rooms. While the china was displayed in several rooms, his china closet was enormous. It may have contained the pieces for use. I noticed Boye & Dresden. The great banqueting hall for the retainers in the olden time was enormous. Flags and ornaments helped its appearance. On each side of the Castle ran small halls 88 feet in length, filled with trophies of the chase, most of them marked with the names of the man who had killed, with the date, etc. There were hundreds of them. Opening into these long narrow halls were rooms used, I suppose, for guests, perhaps servants. The Castle was lighted by electricity and the Duke replied to Laura's question as to how it was heated, by saying it was not heated, "We freeze." The fireplaces were very small. The walls were enormous. The oldest, built in 1200 & something I measured with my cane & found to be over 9 feet thick. That built 200 years later was a little less thick. The Duke said they knew of several secret stairways in the older parts of the walls. We lunched at the little hotel opposite the park, a good lunch & after change of trains arrived at Inverness & stopped at the Caladonian overnight, then motored by Loch Ness to Fort Augustus on yesterday afternoon. The scenery of the lake is fine, but trees affect the view from the road. It is a very narrow road & for 3 motorists to pass is dangerous. We felt a thrill in passing one as ours came close to the edge of a high cliff & we received a bit of the feeling we should have had if we had tumbled off. We passed the night at the "Lorat Arms." Vile hotel. I saw Lord Astor's shooting lodge sitting high above us on the mountain as I dressed & looked out."

ABOUT THE AUTHOR

Laura Blair Marvel was born in 1922 in New York City. She moved to the home of her uncle and aunt, the Blairs, who lived in Blair House in Washington DC when she was 4 years old. She was subsequently formally adopted by the Blairs and enjoyed a privileged childhood and adolescence in the exquisite Blair House. After graduating from the exclusive Foxcroft School, in Virginia, Laura Blair Marvel assumed at a very tender age, dual roles as both hostess for her uncle at Blair House and as social secretary of the Order of the Society of Cincinnati. She married Ted Boggs, moved to Charleston, SC. And raised 5 boys. Later, she moved to New Castle, DE, where she met her second husband, William Marvel, Chancellor to the Court of Chancery of Delaware. She now lives at Stonegates, a retirement in Greenville, DE.

CPSIA information can be obtained at www.ICGtesting.com
Printed in the USA
LVOW08s2156121113

361035LV00001B/262/A